WHAT OTHERS ARE SAYING ABOUT THIS BOOK

"Everyone needs to be strategic. My friend, Dr. Bernie, makes it easy to understand and do—instantly!"
—Mark Victor Hansen, co-author, *Chicken Soup for the Soul*

"This exciting book is a hands-on, principle-centered approach to success. Complete the worksheets, pay the price, and you will make a significant difference in your life and in the world."
—Dr. Stephen R. Covey, author, *The 7 Habits of Highly Effective People* and *The 8th Habit: From Effectiveness to Greatness*

"Everyone is born with a range of abilities unique to him or her. It's fair to say that these abilities are essentially your core strengths. Dr. Bernie has written a wonderful guide on how to get the most out of your life by tapping into vast reservoirs of talent. Armed with this knowledge, you will be able to avoid stress and achieve satisfaction throughout all areas of life!"
—Gary Ryan Blair, The GoalsGuy

"This book will help you sort out your experiences and dreams, assess what truly matters in your own life, and illuminate your path toward a richer and more meaningful existence. Take the first step to changing your life - get this book, develop a new life strategy, and then act on it!"
—Burt Nanus, author of *Visionary Leadership* and *Leaders Who Make a Difference*

"Dr. Dahl wrote the book I wish I had written! Read it; use it; and don't loan it out (because you won't get it back) This book and its accompanying CD-ROM will make the process easier and more productive for you than any book of its type that I know (including my own)."
—George Morrisey, author of *Creating Your Future: Personal Strategic Planning for Professionals* and the *Morrisey on Planning* series

"This is a solid book filled with helpful information for anyone who wants to strategically enhance their business and their life."
—Nido Qubein, author of *Stairway to Success* and *How to Be a Great Communicator*

MORE...

"Many, many people are interested in better ways of reaching their goals and will appreciate this addition to the literature of achievement ... anyone who sticks with the book and follows its instructions will certainly end up with some improvements to his or her ability to meet life's many demands."
—G. Miki Hayden, *Writer's Digest 11th Annual Self-Published Book Awards*

"A wonderfully honest and soul-searching book. It's a page-turner!"
—Thomas Gaffey, M.D., Mayo Clinic

"The book is great! ... Well-written, interesting concept, great references, and excellent use of quotes to support and clarify points throughout."
—Krista Michelle Arrigo, *Succeed Magazine*

"Dr. Dahl has created an interesting and straightforward perspective on the value of strategic planning."
—James Delamater, President and CEO, Northeast Bank

"A method to simplify laying out the road map to one's future, even for the most recalcitrant among us."
—Lawrence Peterson, CPA, President, Torrey Consulting

"If you want to give meaning to your life, read this book."
—Edward G. Pickett, newspaper publisher

"A most helpful book to energize one's inner power to succeed; full of direct, no-nonsense, good common sense and simple wisdom."
—Chungliang Al Huang, Living Tao Foundation, author of *Quantum Soup*

"What a find! ... Coaching is based on the use of powerful questions and this book is loaded with them. The book is well-written and easy to read ... Aside from the focus on personal planning, one of the added benefits of this book is the supportive material on values and visioning included ... provides a solid foundation for the personal strategic planning process. *The worksheets at the end of each chapter are, by themselves, worth the price of the book.* Potential readers should not view the One Page Strategic Plan as being simplistic. If done according to Dr. Dahl's instructions, the planning process will require some effort and a whole lot of thought."
—William McPeck, Coach/Consultant

MORE...

"Some people talk about management, but have never done it. Some people have done it, without knowing how. Here is a how to from one who has done it well."
—James Navin, M.D., Hawaii

"This is a get-involved book, almost a workbook, with charts and self-evaluation sections … the author certainly has a sense of humor. The book is very enjoyable to read."
—PMA Benjamin Franklin Awards

"As an accountant, I am familiar with providing a 'one page' summary,' hence my attraction to the book ... I had no idea of the depth of the material expressed so well yet in such simple terms."
—Warwick Suter, Springfield, Queensland, Australia

"Your book is thin and lightweight; however, the message is not… the questions raised are heavyweight. The book is thought-provoking. Many times I reflected on 'what could or should have been.' The book may be thin and lightweight to carry around, but the points raised are not. Being honest with one's self in answering some of the questions is tough."
—Joe Plandowski, Lakewood Consulting

"It's often been said that one must first 'get one's own house in order.' This book is an amazing tool for analyzing oneself from the inner core of basic values and self image and worth. It leads one through the process of taking charge of one's life, determining short and long term goals and setting a course for attaining them. Well worth the investment of time and money. Life changing."
—John Bragg, President, N.H. Bragg

To: Tinner
All the best!
Bernie Dahl, M.D.

Optimize Your Life!

INTERACTIVE WORKSHEETS CD EDITION

Bernhoff A. Dahl, M.D.

APELLICON-PEARSON PRESS

A division of
Trionics International, Inc.
Winterport, Maine, USA
www.TrionicsUSA.com/oyl

Optimize Your Life! Interactive Worksheets CD Edition
Copyright © 2005 by Bernhoff A. Dahl, M.D.

Published by

A division of Trionics International, Inc.
66 Upper Oak Point Winterport, ME 04496 USA
or
PO Box 271 Hampden, ME 04444 USA
www.TrionicsUSA.com

Library of Congress Cataloging-in-Publication Data

Dahl, Bernhoff A., 1938-
   Optimize your life! : interactive worksheets CD edition / by Bernhoff A. Dahl.--
[Rev. ed.].
      p. cm.
   Rev. ed. of: Optimize your life with the one-page strategic planner. c2003.
   Includes bibliographical references and index.
   ISBN 0-936232-06-4 (pbk. : alk. paper)
1. Success--Psychological aspects. 2. Planning--Psychological aspects. 3. Goal
(Psychology) I. Dahl, Bernhoff A., 1938- Optimize your life with the one-page stra-
tegic planner. II. Title.

   BF637.S8D26 2005
   158.1--dc22

                        2004029178

ISBN 0-936232-06-4
Printed in the United States of America
by McNaughton & Gunn 960 Woodland Drive Saline, MI 48176

This book is dedicated to

YOU

**for you can be the master of your life,
the hero of your quest.**

*"For what shall it profit a man, if he shall gain
the whole world and lose his own soul?"*
—Jesus of Nazareth

This book is based on the premise that

YOU

**are the center of your universe;
you need to first take care of yourself,
then you may better relate to others.**

*"...place the mask on your face
before assisting others."*
—American Airlines

Apologia Pro Libro Suo

This book uses the weakness of mere words to share the power of
focused and simplified *personal* strategic planning.
To compensate, I have taken the liberty of using too many
italics and Capitals.

"'She's quite incredibly literary, you know—quite fantastically!'
*I remember his saying of her that **she felt in italics***
***and thought in capitals**."*
—Henry James, *The Figure in the Carpet*

However, *The One-page Strategic Planner* has worked for me.
I hope it will work for you.

SPECIAL PRICING

This book is available at a volume discount for educational use, employee gifts, sales promotions, premiums, fund-raising, or reselling.
Custom-printed editions, too.

ATTENTION LITERARY AGENTS AND PUBLISHERS

This book has been licensed for translation and publication in a
number of countries outside of the USA. Contact us at
info@trionicsusa.com for information regarding
availability in other countries.

Preface to the Second Edition

While the concept of "The One-page Strategic Planner" was the basis for decades of my *personal* strategic planning, it was first applied in 1981 as *organizational* strategic planning in the real-life situation of my medical group practice. During the next two decades, the concept was adapted to over one hundred consulting projects, keynote addresses, and workshops addressing *both* personal and organizational strategic planning. It became evident to me that personal and organization strategic planning were one in the same.

During this time, I met Charles E. Dwyer, Ph.D., at The Wharton School at the University of Pennsylvania, who added credence to this conclusion. He noted that:

> *"Organizations do not have, never have had, never will have, indeed cannot have: objectives, goals, missions, visions, ideals, ideologies, or philosophies."*

Therefore, I concluded:

> *"Organizational strategic planning is in effect the merging of the personal strategic planning of the key individuals involved in the organization."*

In 2003 I published the first edition of *Optimize Your Life! The One-page Strategic Planner,* which focused on personal strategic planning but was designed to be readily adapted to organizational strategic planning—be it for an organization in a business, church, social club, education… virtually every aspect of human endeavor.

Much has happened since the book was released. I learned a great deal about the dynamic and competitive world of book publishing. During this short time I have:

- enjoyed unprecedented worldwide sales via my distributor, Biblio Distribution, to wholesalers such as Ingram and Baker & Taylor to bookstores in the USA and Canada, the major online booksellers, as well as directly on my own web site and through my keynotes and workshops
- made significant changes and updates for this second edition, primarily by the addition of the Interactive Worksheets CD (which also includes an e-book). Special appreciation is extended to our computer software expert Susan Goodwin,

who extensively beta-tested the Interactive Worksheets, and to David Fitzpatrick, who designed them (and did the layout for this book).

- received great support from Ron Crane at Furbush-Roberts Printing and Shaun Gargan at Bacon Printing, both in Maine, in the production of galleys
- been fortunate to have received a host of enthusiastic endorsements from bestselling authors such as Dr. Stephen R. Covey (*The 7 Habits of Highly Effective People*), Mark Victor Hansen (*Chicken Soup for the Soul*), and Gary Ryan Blair (*The GoalsGuy*). I especially enjoyed the heartfelt endorsement by George Morrisey, a major writer in the world of strategic planning, when he said, "Dr. Dahl wrote the book I wish I had written."
- enjoyed great written reviews and TV and radio coverage
- licensed the book to publishers in Korea (Success Times Publishing), Japan (Discover 21), India (Tata McGraw-Hill), Mainland China (China WaterPower Press), and with Random House Mondadori of Barcelona, Spain, for a worldwide Spanish edition. Negotiations with a host of other publishers is well underway

Above all, I have been encouraged by the thousands of people I have been able to reach with my simple message, and for the number who have written or emailed me with uplifting messages of appreciation such as:

"Your book has changed my life!"

—Bernie Dahl, M.D.
Winterport, Maine, USA
Summer 2005

Acknowledgements

"Finish that book before you start another project!" That would have been the advice of my dear departed father.

Yes, Dad; this book is not only finished, it is a book about finishing—about defining one's dreams and finishing them.

Although the concept of *The One-page Strategic Planner* originated many years ago, it was gelled in 1981 in our group medical practice. I received support and advice from Robert J. Malvesta, M.D., Terrance O'Callahan, M.D., John S. Kaiser, M.D., and Mark Illingworth, M.B.A. At that time, the concept was also applied at Overhead Door Company of Maine, with the help of my co-owner, Mark Talon.

During the subsequent two decades, the concept was applied, tested, and improved in a wide range of settings, including keynotes and workshops with a number of regional and national organizations and associations.

I would like to thank the many clients with whom I have applied the concept "in the trenches" of the dynamic and competitive world of business and professional ventures. I must acknowledge the powerful insights that I gained at the feet of the iconoclastic guru of strategic planning, Henry Mintzberg in Canada.

As the idea of this book emerged, I received support from Dan Poynter of Santa Barbara, as well as Mark Victor Hansen of the *Chicken Soup for the Soul* book series. I also gained great insights and encouragement from the many teachers at the University of South Florida's Suncoast Writers Conference (Dr. Steven J. Rubin) and the Santa Barbara Writers Conference (Barnaby Conrad and Cork Milner).

During the completion of the book, I received valuable input from Krista Michelle Arrigo, Erin Campbell, Pauline Kaiser, Ph.D., David Platt, Joni Ramsay, and Michael Talbert, M.D. Additional support was received from Andrew Grossman, Merrideth Miller, and Mary Suggett, all of whom helped us select comics and cartoons.

Of greatest support was David M. Fitzpatrick, who worked in my writing studio for months and valiantly fought for proper grammar and syntax, and against the abuse of *italics* and Capitals.

Contents

Is This Book For You?

This book is for ME because...
Optimize Your Life! works for me
I wish to share its power with others

This book is for YOU if you wish to...
° Develop an overview of your life
° Gain insights about yourself
° Address your roles in life
° Define a successful life
° Help you prioritize
° Take charge of your life
° Eliminate "toxic" forces/people
° Value yourself first
° Define your resources
° Analyze your values and their power
° Clean up your clutter
° Take advantage of opportunities
° Define and meet challenges
° Enjoy what you have, do, and are
° Address your risk tolerance or aversion
° Make wise choices
° Evaluate your wants *versus* needs
° Simplify your life
° Learn to live "in the moment"
° **Optimize, not maximize, your life**
° **Become a better person**
° **Have more fun**
° **...and optimize your organization as well**

"Cui dono lepidum novum libellum
Arido modo pumice expolitum
(Here's my small book out, nice and new,
Fresh-bound—whom shall I give it to?) *"*
—Catullus

Optimize Your Life! is a self-development system that features a process for defining, accepting, and improving YOU. This system may work for you regardless of your age, sex, race, social status, education, talents, resources, beauty, ability to learn, old habits, health, etc.

The materials in this book, including text and worksheets, can be readily adapted for strategic planning for an organization, be it in the world of business, religion, education, social services, etc.

WARNING

This book is not a substitute for professional help, be it legal, medical, psychological, religious, etc., when needed. There are many other books to augment this book in your search for an optimized life.

In orthopedic surgery, we learned the aphorism "Splints designed to fit all patients rarely fit any patient." However, this book is designed to be flexible enough to meet the *personal* strategic planning needs of most people. The person who reads and applies the concepts of this book will need to adapt the worksheets to his own *personal* environment and needs.

Optimize Your Life! may grab you and change your life. It may provide a framework on which you can build, create, develop, and accomplish a more powerful and successful strategic plan for your life.

"The ideas I stand for are not mine.
I borrowed them from Socrates,
I swiped them from Chesterfield,
I stole them from Jesus."
—Dale Carnegie

"Me too, Dale."

How To Use This Book

Optimize Your Life! is a "how-to" book, complete with text to read and examples to ponder. There are many worksheets on which to write, answer questions, make choices, select goals and projects, and define specific tasks in your new life. However, to complete the cycle of strategic planning, one must act, one must implement those carefully-selected tasks.

There are five *phases* to achieve the maximal success for the use of this book:

1. **Read it!**
   Read all the text and examples.
2. **Think about it!**
   Think about the questions and answers.
3. **Write it!**
   Write down your responses on the worksheets.
4. **Do it!**
   Do your chosen tasks.
5. **Celebrate it!**
   Celebrate your efforts and achievements.

Read the text and complete the worksheets at a comfortable pace. Some areas call for rapid-fire creative "brainstorming," others for thoughtful and careful deliberation.

After your first pass through the book and worksheets, you will be encouraged to repeat the process of reading and updating the worksheets. Revisit your questions and answers and even create new questions to be answered, refine or select new goals, projects, and tasks. Implement these new tasks. Celebrate your efforts, successful or not. Learn from frustration and failures. Redefine the course. Continue the race. Make *Optimize Your Life!* a habit, a lifestyle, the cornerstone of your new examined and successful life.

The point of view of this book is simple:
We start out together, then focus on *you*.
This book is *your* book. The focus is on *you*.

Since you will be dealing with sensitive information about yourself and your world, you may wish to create an environment of privacy. You may choose to photocopy the individual worksheets and complete and update them. For privacy's sake, you may wish to use a simple lockbox.

Since this edition offers an Interactive Worksheets CD, it is far easier to enter, edit, update, and print out your personal planning, and maintain privacy through password protection of your work.

In addition, you may include another individual or even several benevolent and qualified persons. They can serve as mentors or coaches to assist you. You may wish to include a healthcare professional such as a physician or psychologist, or a religious leader such as a rabbi, minister, imam, or priest.

You may use this book to simply address a few issues in your life or you may wish to reread and revisit it to optimize all aspects of your life. You may, however, wish to go deeper into yourself and your world and how you make choices—the ultimate Journey into the Self.

There will be no test—no exams—during or after the use of this book and the employment of the principles of *Optimize Your Life!* Your new life will be the ultimate test.

Once again, you can adapt the text and worksheets in this book for organizational strategic planning.

I trust you will earn an "A" for effort and success!

"Whoever would know himself,
let him open a book."
—Jean Paulhan

"A book that furnishes no quotations is,
me judice, *no book—it is a plaything."*
—Thomas Love Peacock

The Power of Questions:
The Building Blocks of *Optimize Your Life!*

"Truth fears no questions."
—Anonymous

Greek philosophers since the age of Thales (624?-546? B.C.) followed by Socrates, Plato, and Aristotle, have used questions as the driving force of philosophy... the search for understanding and truth.

The "Top 10" Personal Questions
1. Who am I?
2. What am I doing now?
3. What do I value?
4. What am I good at?
5. What are my passions in life?
6. What is a "successful" life to me?
7. What are the "toxic" forces in my life?
8. What do I want to have/do/be in life?
9. What is my risk tolerance?
10. What do I need to do to "clean up" my life?

These same questions can be adapted for an organization:

The "Top 10" Organizational Questions
1. What is the organization?
2. What is the organization doing now?
3. What does the organization value?
4. What is the organization good at?
5. What are the organization's passions?
6. What is a "successful" organization?
7. What are the "toxic" forces in/out of the organization?
8. What does the organization want to have/do/be?
9. What is the organization's risk tolerance?
10. What must the organization do to "clean up" itself?

These generic questions lead to personalized questions, which, in turn, beget new questions, and on and on...

"To solve any problem, here are three questions to ask yourself:
First, What could I do?
Second, What could I read?
And third, Who could I ask?"
—Jim Rohn

Rabbinical student: Rabbi, rabbi, why do you always answer a question with a question?
Rabbi: Is there another way?

"I no longer seek all the answers
But merely to understand the questions better."
—The wisdom of kung fu

"The most important questions in life can never be answered by anyone except one's self."
—John Fowles, English novelist

"Our minds, bodies, feelings, relationships
are all informed by our questions...
What you ask is who you are.
What you find depends on what you search for...
And what shapes our lives are the questions we ask,
refuse to ask, or never think of asking."
—Sam Keen, philosopher and theologian,
adapted from *Spirituality & Health,* Spring 2000

Above all...
"Ask an impertinent question,
get a pertinent answer."
—Agent Fox Mulder, *The X-Files*

Introduction

"When you come to a fork in the road, take it."
—Yogi Berra

Classic Strategic Planning

In this age of rapid change and uncertainty, replete with untold challenges and opportunities, every organization, every business, and every person needs a game plan, a compass, a road map; that is, *everybody needs a strategic plan.*

Since prehistoric times, some level of planning, albeit primitive, has played a key role in the survival and success of humankind. Formal or informal, even at a subconscious level, planning has been applied to a wide range of human endeavors from hunting and gathering, to farming, trade, exploration and military excursions.

Strategic planning has proven to be a powerful management tool for one's business or professional life. In its most basic form, strategic planning:

- sets direction
- allocates resources
- evaluates alternatives

Introducing *The One-page Strategic Planner*

The One-page Strategic Planner is a simplified and focused process adapting classic strategic planning for a wide range of applications including personal use. Classic strategic planning reduces the selected Goals down to Focused Action Plans to be implemented.

The One-page Strategic Planner simplifies this entire process by further reducing Focused Action Plans down to their component Projects and then to irreducible Focused Tasks. Each of these Focused Tasks is assigned to *one page,* wherein ten key questions are asked and answered, as indicated below.

Questions posed on *The One-page Strategic Planner*
1. What is the specific Task?
2. What is the current status?
3. What is the definition of success?
4. Who will do it? (champions and team)
5. What will the champion and team specifically do?
6. What resources are needed/lacking?
7. What specific challenges/hurdles are expected?
8. When will the task be done?
9. How will progress, success, or failure be evaluated and measured?
10. Who will monitor the progress and to whom will the reports be given?

The term "champion" comes from the world of organizational strategic planning. The champion is the leader of a team assigned to the project. In personal strategic planning, you are the champion.

While there are many worksheets in this book, the *One-page* concept deals with your irreducible Focused Tasks.

The Author's World of Strategic Thinking and Planning

After earning a degree in Chemistry, I went on to Cornell University for an M.D. degree. Next I completed an internship and residency in pathology at the University of Vermont. To meet my military obligations, I served as an Epidemic Intelligence Service Officer with the Center for Disease Control in Atlanta. Fresh out of the CDC, I was named as the Chief of Pathology at a medical center in New England at the tender age of 33.

It was an opportunity of a lifetime. I co-founded a medical group, using the organizational design of synergy (equality and sharing) instead of classic hierarchy. The awesome power of synergy carried us successfully along for almost a decade.

In 1981, I developed a one-page plan entitled by an acronym: "WIAFDIHIDLOY/M" ("When it all falls down, I hope it doesn't land on you or me"). This one-page strategic plan addressed the "crises" our group was experiencing as we expanded into the increasingly complex and competitive world of healthcare. The plan listed specific potential crises, their immediate or long-term effects, and how each might be neutralized or minimized in the present or in the future. This planning process, which augmented the organizational power of color-coded file cabinets and three-ring notebooks of my youth, served us well for several years.

Eventually, I was introduced to full-fledged strategic planning and became addicted to its grand form. After adding the concept of the power of *values*, I created my own version, the six step *Values-driven Strategic Thinking and Planning*. I shared my insights as a lecturer and consultant. Included in these six steps are the creation of Values, Mission, and Vision Statements, followed by SWOT analysis (*internal* strengths and weaknesses, *external* opportunities and threats) and selection of Goals and Plans (often referred to as Focused Action Plans). The last step is Implementation or the "do it" phase. This six-step process was arranged in a hexagon motif.

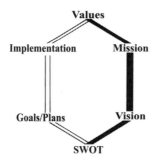

For several decades, I have served as either a participant, observer, consultant, or facilitator of strategic planning projects in over one hundred professional and business settings nationwide. Some of these projects led to laudable successes. These planning projects were, however, costly in time, energy, emotions, and money, and generated lengthy reports—often never used.

As a result of these experiences, I sought a simpler, focused, or "minimalist" approach to strategic planning. Upon my retirement from the full-time practice of Medicine in 1995, I re-visited the one-page plan of 1981 and developed *Optimize Your Life! The One-page Strategic Planner.*

While the *One-page* planner is a variation on the theme of classic strategic planning, it places most of the effort on a limited number of specific tasks—each of which *can be reduced to one page!* Unlike the bulky, computer-driven boilerplate reports produced by many strategic planners, the *One-page* adaptation can be readily understood, mastered, and applied in a wide range of venues. The process first addresses the *Goals* of the organization,

GOAL

Projects

Focused Tasks

then focuses on the components of the Goals—specific *Projects.* Next, each Project is reduced to even smaller specific Focused Tasks.

By reducing strategic planning to its smallest and most manageable units—Tasks—the chances of successful Implementation are much greater. Since success breeds more success, each small but successful advance brings support for strategic planning, and the cycle can be repeated with other tasks and other projects, until the larger goals are reached.

Over the past decade, *Optimize Your Life!* has been modified and improved with the help of many organizations, associations,

and academic institutions. First, it was successfully applied in business and professional activities. Subsequently, it was adapted for *personal* strategic planning.

During the application and field testing of the concepts in this book, it became evident that personal and organizational strategic planning were, in fact, one in the same. This was based on my own observations in the field and was later supported by Charles M. Dwyer, Ph.D., who noted:

> *"Organizations do not have, never have had, never will have, indeed cannot have: objectives, goals, missions, visions, ideals, ideologies, or philosophies."*

Therefore, one can conclude:

> *"Organizational strategic planning is, in effect, the merging of the personal strategic planning of the key individuals involved in the organization."*

As a result, the text and the worksheets can be readily adapted from personal strategic planning, the primary focus of this book, to organizational strategic planning.

—Bernhoff A. Dahl, M.D.
Winterport, Maine, USA

> *Failing to plan may well be planning to fail.*

*"He who every morning plans the transactions of the day,
and follows that plan, carries a thread that will guide him
through the labyrinth of the most busy life.*

*The orderly arrangement of this time is like
a ray of light which darts itself through all
his occupations.*

*But where no plan is laid, where the disposal of time
is surrendered merely to the chance of
incidents, all things lie huddled together
in one chaos, which admits of neither
distribution nor review."*

—Victor Hugo

Impatient? Want to jump right in?
Can't wait for the introductory database?
Why not try out the "One-page?"
How about something whimsical in your life that you would like to:

- Finish a lingering project... complete a stamp collection
- Improve or master... in your golf game, your putting
- Create something special... bake a great soufflé
- Gain a skill... play the flute
- Other...

Jump to page 131 and try out the "One-page" concept!

Part I

Strategic Planning Overview

"The best laid schemes o' mice and men oft go astray."
—Robert Burns, *To A Mouse,* 1785

Alice: Which way should I go?

Cheshire Cat: That depends on
where you are going.

Alice: I don't know
where I am going!

Cheshire Cat: Then it doesn't
matter which way you go!

—Lewis Carroll, *Alice's
Adventures in Wonderland*, 1872

Chapter 1

What Is Personal Strategic Planning?

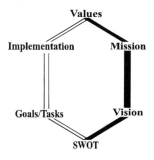

Chapter 1
What is Personal Strategic Planning?

"The unexamined life is not worth living."
—Socrates

Life is a journey, not a destination; it is a process, not an end point. A truly examined life can be a journey into self-discovery: a Journey into the Self.

For some, life is viewed as a time of many opportunities and too many choices. For others, life is a struggle with challenges and frustrations. For a select few, life is not a problem to be overcome but a mystery to be explored—perhaps even solved. Personal strategic planning, by using its powerful and penetrating questions, can provide a life-long technique or process to deal with the "cards one was dealt." It may help the practitioner to optimize one's life—to get the best out of life, not simply the most out of life.

For some, *personal* strategic planning may be a process that focuses on identifying and eliminating "toxic" people and forces from their lives. For others, it will serve to address crises; for others, opportunities. For some, strategic planning will be an ongoing way of life—a lifestyle by which they constantly update and address their goals and celebrate their efforts and successes.

The History of Organizational Strategic Planning

The story of formal strategic planning started some 10,000 years ago, at the beginning of the Neolithic Age, in the Karakadag Mountains of southeastern Turkey. With the planting of *einkorn* (a primitive variety of wheat), the Agricultural Revolution began. Humans had been competing with other, often faster and larger, animals in a world of hunting and gathering. *Homo sapiens* were just another animal except for two key items in their toolkit: the ability to communicate with words; and the ability to think, reason, and plan for the future.

In the intervening ten millennia, all human progress and civilization has been linked to this ability to plan: to collect and store seeds, to select and till the soil, and to plant, nurture, harvest, preserve, and process food. Along with animal husbandry, this deliberate modification of ecosystems permitted a massive increase in human population. It also allowed individuals and society the time and stability to specialize in developing ideas, concepts, products, and services.

Over these hundred centuries, there have been many periods of human endeavor and achievement that have been linked with strategic planning. During the Industrial Revolution of the nineteenth century and the two World Wars in the twentieth, strategic planning has played a key role in meeting the demands of industry. Formal strategic planning has resulted in great successes as well as dismal failures, from multinational corporations like General Electric to the politically-driven disasters of the Communists in the former Soviet Union.

While strategic planning addresses the future, it cannot predict it. It can assist in dealing with some aspects of our world of accelerated change and instability which are driven by a number of dynamic forces:

- Technological advances
- Telecommunications
- The "Global Village"
- International competition
- Multinational corporations and ventures
- Instability of organizations
- Time-based rapid competition
- Worldwide excess industrial capacity
- The threat of economic depression
- Increased consumer expectations
- Government intervention (laws/regulations)
- The power of diversity
- Population explosion and shift
- Changes in values

Many aspects of these changes may also apply to one's personal life. When successfully applied, strategic planning has accelerated many of these changes. It is ironic to note that while strategic planning has solved many problems, it has also created new challenges and revealed countless opportunities.

What is Strategic Planning?

In *Applied Strategic Planning,* Goodstein, Nolan, and Pfeiffer offer the following definition:

"The process by which the guiding members of an organization envision its future and develop the necessary procedure and operations to achieve the future."

A very simple definition might be

"Strategic planning is the management of the future."

Strategic planning and its Implementation in its broadest sense can be divided into four components, wherein:

1. **Planning** is the *analysis* of the situations
2. **Strategy** is the *synthesis* of the solutions
3. **Setting Goals** is the *targeting*
4. **Implementation** is *operational* and employs *tactics.*

The analysis and synthesis of strategic planning yield the strategies that define the goals that describe "what should be done." Implementation is the operational aspect of action that focuses on "how to get the tasks done."

Adapting full-scale strategic planning to *personal* use is both simple and complex. It is simple in that we are dealing largely with just one individual and his life. But it is complex in that the process goes deeper into the mystical values and motivation of the individual and deals with the complexities of his world. The focus and questions of the strategic planning process have to be changed from the third person plural to the second person singular ("you") and then on to the first person singular ("I" and "me").

One of the challenges of *personal* strategic planning is that data collection, analysis, and decision-making are usually more successful when addressed by a small team. To correct this situation, an individual pursuing *personal* strategic planning can gain support and wisdom by adding professionals or benevolent people to his efforts.

Optimize Your Life! will guide you to look at the parts of "you" in detail—to *analyze* you and your world—from several vantage points. It will then reassemble you in different ways—to *synthesize* you and your world—and weave a series of potential tapestries of the new "you." Based on these steps, observations, and results, you will define and set Goals (targeting) for your "examined" life, followed by their implementation.

This process may be divided into five *phases*:
1. Know yourself
2. Know your world
3. Make wise choices
4. Live an examined life
5. Celebrate your efforts and successes

Optimize Your Life! will use and adapt all of the steps of the author's time-tested *Values-driven Strategic Thinking and Planning* format for *organizations* as follows:
1. **Know yourself:** Creating your Values, Mission, and Vision Statements. Addressing your *internal* Strengths and Weaknesses (the SW in SWOT)
2. **Know your world:** Addressing your *external* Opportunities and Threats (the OT in SWOT)
3. **Make wise choices:** Defining Goals, Projects, and Focused Tasks, using the task-based One-page Strategic Planner
4. **Live an examined life:** Implementing and using *Optimize Your Life!* as a lifestyle
5. **Celebrate your efforts and successes:** Living the *Optimize Your Life!* lifestyle successfully

We are reminded of the words of Rudyard Kipling,
"I kept six honest serving-men (They taught me all I knew); Their names are What and Why and When And How and Where and Who."

We can apply these same key words to *Optimize Your Life!:*

- **Who** should plan? All who want to optimize their Lives—especially you.
- **What** should you plan? The key aspects of your Life—the most important things first.
- **When** should you plan? Daily, weekly, monthly, yearly—continuously update.
- **Where** should you plan? Continuously "think it" … "write it" when you can … always "do it."
- **Why** should you plan? Because there are countless rewards and benefits, great and small.
- **How** should you plan? Use *Optimize Your Life!* as a life-style.

The *Optimize Your Life!* book can be used in a variety of ways, including an initial general overview of your life. It can then be adapted and focused on a wide range of challenges or opportunities, such as planning for specific aspects of:

- Educational opportunities, both short- and long-term, as well as lifelong learning
- Career choices such as the military, a new job, a sabbatical leave, or an early retirement
- Personal relationships that are formal, informal, or even intimate
- Rearing of super kids
- Examining and expanding your spiritual life
- Eliminating "toxic" people and forces
- Recreation, including sports and travel
- Health concerns such as weight control, smoking cessation, genetic dispositions to disease
- Major purchases, sales, or gifts
- Starting or expanding your own business venture
- Learning to play a musical instrument or to speak a foreign language

Author's Suggestions

As you progress through this book, reading the text and writing in the worksheets, you have two major choices.

1. You can move rapidly, addressing only the highlights on the worksheets, filling in the easy parts. In the process, you may focus on very specific challenges or opportunities in your current life. You may wish to define and select short-term goals that deal with:

   a. Impending crises that may escalate

   b. Negative or "toxic" forces in your life

   c. Transient opportunities that may disappear

2. You can go slowly and deliberately, completing all the worksheets in each chapter before moving on—but move fast enough so you do not lose momentum.

> *"Thinking well is wise; planning well is wiser;*
> *but doing well is the wisest and best of all."*
> —Persian proverb

> *"You've got to be very careful if you don't know where*
> *you're going, because you might not get there."*
> —Yogi Berra

Optimize Your Life!
Quick Results

To assist you in gaining early success, a Quick Results box like this one is included at the ends of many of the chapters. After all, it is a human attribute that "success breeds success"
...the earlier the better.

Part II

The Strategy of
Personal Planning

"To boldly go where no man has gone before."
—From the Starfleet Charter

"Look well into thyself; there is a source of strength which will always spring up if thou wilt always look there."
—Marcus Aurelius Antoninus

Chapter 2

Who Are You?

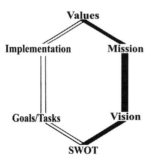

*"What lies behind us and what lies before us
are tiny matters compared to what lies within us."*
—Ralph Waldo Emerson

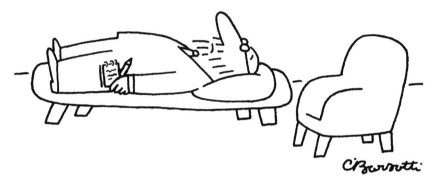

Know yourself.

Chapter 2
Who Are You?
Defining a brief personal inventory

"Know yourself."
—The Oracle of Delphi

Who Are You?

This book, based on the power of questions, opens with the most important question in your life: "Who are you?" As you answer this and other questions, new questions will arise for you to ponder, puzzle out, and write down.

You are a unique product of the cosmos. No one else in the universe, past or present, has your exact genetic makeup unless you are an identical twin. Even if you are an identical twin, you will still be special in matters of the mind and soul. You have been given the greatest gift of all: the gift of life.

The next key question in this book will be:
"What will you do with the gift of your life?"

Asking Yourself Questions

Since the dawn of time, humans have pondered that greatest of all personal questions: "Who am I?" From the literature of the East, such as Lao Tzu's book *Tao Te Ching,* to that of the West, such as Aristotle's *Nicomachean Ethics,* we read of humanity in its adaptation to its world.

We can start with current popular literature, with a book appropriately entitled *Who Am I?,* edited by Robert Frager, Ph.D. The book details classifying humans into eight general systems and twenty-eight specific type categories. They range from the mystical to the tangible, from astrological types to body typologies, as well as personality types, ranging from those in Eastern traditions to psychological typologies which include concepts from Freud, Erikson, Horney, Jung, and others. The successful use of *Optimize Your Life!* draws from the wisdom of the ages, including the history of humanity, philosophy, religion, and psychology.

Focusing on Body, Mind, and Soul

In our efforts, we will follow the lead of the ancient Greeks who advised us to view ourselves from three vantage points: *body, mind, and soul.*

Addressing your body type and its current status is relatively easy, for your body is exceedingly tangible and readily identified, examined, and defined. However, dealing with your mind—your intellect—is more difficult.

Your mind is more mystical. In the world of education and academics, there are a host of tests to measure intellect. The challenge of defining your soul, spirit, or psyche is greater, for that world is one of pure mystery.

The concepts and teachings at this level of our being, over the past three millennia, have been presented and preserved in many great books and morphed into personality and psychological testing "instruments." To keep your efforts in addressing "Who am I?" simple, unbiased, and fun, I have avoided such material (see Appendix for Internet sources).

Diogenes walked the streets of ancient Athens, carrying a lantern as he searched for an honest man. This book is, metaphorically, Diogenes' lantern, providing light for you to better look honestly into your being.

Enjoy the adventure.

Brainstorming

It is now time to do a bit of thinking followed by some writing in the first worksheet at the end of this chapter. We will start with a mind-expanding, brainstorming, and fun exercise as we fill in the blanks of Worksheet 2.1, "Who am I? A Brainstorming Personal View."

You may enter anything that comes to mind that, in any way, may define you, such as favorite foods, movies, music or even your dislikes. You may include good friends or evil enemies. You may include joys as well as sorrows. Just go for it!

Highlights of Your Life

Now we will look briefly at some of the important events of your life by completing Worksheet 2.2, "Highlights of My Life."

On the worksheet, you are given some subjects to cover; but you may wish to ignore some or add others on your first pass through the book. Should you need more space, you are welcome to photocopy this sheet (and any other worksheets in this book) before you first write on it. This worksheet is your first encounter with subjects we will soon cover in greater detail, such as education, skills development, and achievements. You can always return to this worksheet to make additions or corrections.

Influential People

Precious few of us live in a vacuum, for as John Donne wrote, "No man is an island." Next, we will go briefly beyond just you by focusing on key individuals in your life. We will address your current or past roles and relationships with them on Worksheet 2.3, "Influential People in My Life."

On that worksheet, you are prompted with a list of possibilities, but again, you can add others. This worksheet will also ask you to define the role you/they play and to rank these people as to their impact on your life, past or present.

This process can be quite intimidating. If you are uncomfortable or unsure about this process of prioritizing, do the best you can. You may choose to return to it later.

Key Questions

Then go on to Worksheet 2.4, "Who am I? Eight Key Questions," which deals with a range of subjects designed to gain additional important insights about you. Many of these questions will appear later to be dealt with in more detail.

Author's Suggestions

Do not get bogged down in minutiae, or worse yet, hung up on negative data, interpretations, or feelings. This "Who Am I?" process should be focused on the facts and be as positive as possible without being dishonest. Much of who you are today, your genetics, your "gifts" or talents, and your early life was out of your control. They were the "cards that you were dealt." How you play those cards is in your control and is your challenge, opportunity, and responsibility to optimize your life.

Many of us have taken personality tests of one sort or another during our education, possibly when applying for employment or during military service. Perhaps the most popular are the Myers-Briggs Personality Type Indicator and the Strong Interest Inventory. See the Appendix for information regarding personality testing, many of which are available over the Internet either free or for a modest fee. To keep our efforts focused and easy, follow the positive and uplifting version of the KISS principle:

Keep It Simple and Smart.

"A happy life is one which is in
accordance with its own nature."
—Seneca

"Don't think you are... know you are."
—Morpheus, *The Matrix*

"Knowing others is wisdom;
Knowing the self is enlightenment.
Mastering others requires force;
Mastering the self needs strength.."
—Lao Tzu, *Tao Te Ching*

"Love not what you are,
but what you may become."
—Miguel de Cervantes

Optimize Your Life!
Quick Results: Who Am I?

In 100 words or less, write down who you are.

I am...

NOTE

Here the worksheets are introduced. The included Interactive Worksheets on the CD will allow you to enter, edit, change, save, print, and password protect all your personal planning. The Interactive Worksheets are form-fillable Adobe PDFs and are a full 8.5" x 11" in size. See the CD for details.

The purchaser of this book may also photocopy the worksheets in the book for personal use. You may wish to enlarge each worksheet when copying.

2.1: WHO AM I?—A *BRAINSTORMING* PERSONAL VIEW

Write down anything that comes to mind about *you*. This can be your likes, dislikes, favorite food, literature, movies, people, cities, schools, sports, religion, hobbies, jobs, skills… anything! If you run out of room, make more copies of this sheet.

2.2: WHO AM I?—HIGHLIGHTS OF MY LIFE

List events of importance in your life. They can be positive or negative. If an event made an impact on you, list it. Some common ideas are presented; add others below.

Birth:

Education:

Skills Development:

Military Service:

Employment:

Marriage/Divorce:

Sports/Recreation:

Business Venture:

Achievements:

Travel:

Illness:

Other:

Other:

Other:

2.3: WHO AM I?—INFLUENTIAL PEOPLE IN MY LIFE

What role and relationships do you have (or have you had) with influential people? Fill in names and, when you're finished, rank them in order of importance—consider effort, emotions, and time, with "1" being the most important.

RANK	PERSON	ROLE

You may wish to consider: parent(s), sibling(s), spouse(s), child(ren), family relative(s), close friend(s), intimate friend(s), employer(s), business associate(s), teacher(s)/mentor(s), etc.

2.4: WHO AM I?—EIGHT KEY QUESTIONS

Answer the eight key questions below.

1. I like/am motivated by

2. I am angered by

3. The things I like about me are

4. The things I do not like about me are

5. The key roles in my life are

6. The "toxic" people/forces in my life are

7. The purpose(s) of my life is/are

8. My ideas of a successful life are

*"If we are to go forward, we must go back
and rediscover those precious* values—
*that all reality hinges on moral foundations
and that all reality has spiritual control."*
—Martin Luther King, Jr.

Chapter 3

What Do You Value?

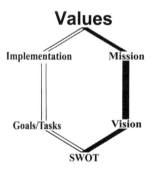

*"Try not to become a man of success but rather
try to become a man of value."*
—Albert Einstein

"Looks like I have a passionate moment open
on the 26th. Should I schedule you?"

Chapter 3
What Do You Value?
Developing a personal Values Statement

*"When your values are clear to you,
making decisions becomes easier."*
—Roy Disney

Your personal values are the center of your universe. Your behavior, every thought you have, every decision you make, every word you utter, every relationship you have with others—everything you do is driven by your values.

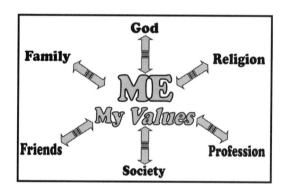

What Are Values?

Values (from the Latin *valere*, to be strong, to be of worth) have been defined in literature, religion, and philosophy to include the widest possible range from eternal ideas to behavioral actions. They are popularly defined as:

*"The acts, customs, institutions, etc. regarded in a
particular (especially favorable) way by a people,
an ethnic group, etc."*

In their purest form, however, values originate and reside at a very deep level in one's soul (psyche) and are, therefore, mystical. In this focused context, values can be defined as:

*"The guidelines and beliefs a person
uses when confronted with a situation
in which a choice is made."*

It is one's behavior that decodes deeper values. Behavior is the only window through which we can judge another person's values—or our own.

$$B = f(V + E)$$

B(Behavior) is a *function* of V(Values) and E(Environment)
Therefore, if you wish to change one's Behavior, and you accept that one's Values are firmly established, you are left with influencing (that is, supporting or threatening) one's Environment.

There is a cynical interpretation of this formula, wherein one's behavior is a function of one's *true* values when he is in an environment where he thinks nobody is watching. This may be the basis of the Las Vegas motto "What happens here... stays here."

The Sources of Values

If values are so important to an individual and his or her behavior, what are the sources of these deep, mystical, powerful forces? The concept and definition of values have been studied for millennia by religious zealots and philosophers, and for the past century by psychologists and social scientists. There is a general consensus that a person gains his values through just a few basic avenues: inculcation, modeling, self-analysis of real-life experiences, and values clarification.

Inculcation: This is the formal or informal teaching by parents, teachers, family members and individuals in our social and religious world during the early formative years of our lives.

Modeling: This is the process by which one selects, on a conscious or subconscious level, important or powerful people in our lives, mentors or "tormentors" (such as bosses, partners, teachers and colleagues) who may serve as role models for our lives and for our values.

Self-analysis of real-life experiences: Major short-term, real-life experiences may cause a person to analyze the situation and formulate, test, and even change his values. Examples include external events such as war, crime, and famine, or internal (personal) events such as divorce, pregnancy, an acute illness, school or business failure, a "religious experience," or an accident. Long-term cumulative experiences such as marriage, child rearing, "empty nest" syndrome, or chronic health problems may be included in a self-evaluation process.

Values clarification: This is a concept fostered by the "humanist movement" in the mid-twentieth century. It approaches the study of values through formal "self- and group-analysis," along with the use of rational thinking and emotional awareness to examine one's behavioral patterns and underlying values. Researchers believe that through a process of "self-actualization," individuals can learn to choose among alternatives and to transcend the limits of their values to some degree.

For most of us, values are:
- Deep and emotional
- Difficult to change
- Sources of strength and stability
- The driving force for our decisions and choices
- The basis for our power to act

Values in History

Modern scholars interested in the study of values have listed almost 100 different human values. The ancient Greek philosopher Aristotle (384-322 BC) described twelve "virtues" which he referred to as "means." He also described twenty-four "vices"; i.e., wherein there was either a lack or an overabundance of any of these virtues.

There is, however, a generally-accepted short list of truly ba-

ARISTOTLE'S NICOMACHEAN ETHICS: TABLE OF VIRTUES AND VICES			
SPHERE OFACTION OR FEELING	**EXCESS**	**MEAN**	**DEFICIENCY**
Fear and Confidence	Rashness	Courage	Cowardice
Pleasure and Pain	Licentiousness/ Self-indulgence	Temperance	Insensibility
Getting and Spending (minor)	Prodigality	Liberality	Illiberality/ Meanness
Getting and Spending (major)	Vulgarity/ Tastelessness	Magnificence	Pettiness/Niggardliness
Honor and Dishonor (major)	Vanity	Magnanimity	Pusillanimity
Honor and Dishonor (minor)	Ambition/empty vanity	Proper ambition/ pride	Unambitiousness/Undue humility
Anger	Irascibility	Patience/Good temper	Lack of spirit/Unirascibility
Self-expression	Boastfulness	Truthfulness	Understatement/Mock modesty
Conversation	Buffoonery	Wittiness	Boorishness
Social Conduct	Obsequiousness	Friendliness	Cantankerousness
Shame	Shyness	Modesty	Shamelessness
Indignation	Envy	Righteous indignation	Malicious enjoyment/ Spitefulness

sic, or *core,* values:

1. Integrity
2. Honesty
3. Fidelity
4. Courage
5. Patience
6. Justice
7. Humility

In his bestseller *The 7 Habits of Highly Effective People*, Stephen R. Covey reviewed the classic literature on values and added temperance, industry, simplicity, and modesty, as well as The Golden Rule. He used the term *Character Ethic* to describe these values as a foundation for success.

Another approach to the study of values is the focus on following certain principles of behavior, such as those listed in the Biblical Ten Commandments, which state:

1. Thou shalt have no other gods before me.
2. Thou shalt not make for yourself graven images.
3. Thou shalt not take the name of the Lord thy God in vain.
4. Remember the sabbath day, and keep it holy.
5. Honor your father and your mother.
6. Thou shalt not kill.
7. Thou shalt not commit adultery.
8. Thou shalt not steal.
9. Thou shalt not bear false witness against thy neighbor.
10. Thou shalt not covet.

These principles are not true values, but rather *behaviors* that are the expression of deeper, underlying values.

It is interesting to note that the oldest set of recorded and preserved laws or principles in the western world predates the Ten Commandments by about 300 years. Babylonian King Hammurabi (1792-1750 BC) codified the 282 detailed laws of Mesopotamia and Sumeria.

Over the millennia, societies have developed laws and regulations, based on underlying values, in order to create and maintain social order and peace. Individual and societal values are also the basis for our concept of ethics and morality. Societal values can be transient and malleable, tending to vary from area to area, and time to time.

Students of values have defined "internal" values, that serve ourselves, such as:

1. Humor
2. Freedom
3. Opportunity
4. Independence
5. Challenge
6. Curiosity

There are also "external" values that focus on our relationships with others and our society, such as:

1. Friendship
2. Sharing
3. Loyalty
4. Acceptance
5. Consideration
6. Love
7. Cooperation

Core Values

On Worksheet 3.1, "Personal Core Values," you are asked to review the seven core values and rate them in order of importance to you. Then, detail why they are important and how you integrate them into your life.

Internal Values

On Worksheet 3.2, "Personal Internal Values," rate your six most common personal internal values. Indicate why they are important and how you integrate them into your life.

External Values

On Worksheet 3.3, "Personal External Values," you will again rate values in order of importance, following with why they are important and how they are integrated into your life.

Values Statement

Worksheet 3.4, "Creating My Values Statement," deals with writing the first draft of your Values Statement. There is also space allocated for you to return later for an update as you learn more about yourself and your world.

Personal Values Checklist

Worksheet 3.5, "Personal Values Checklist," assists you in evaluating your values in your day to day life. The exercise is a "values diary" designed to monitor, in writing, your *values-driven* thoughts, speech, and actions over a one week period. You may wish to photocopy this worksheet in order to take it along with you on your daily journey through life.

Author's Suggestions

Values are important in our lives. They may also be the source of great consternation when we are confronted with major crises or choices.

"Happiness is that state of consciousness which proceeds from the achievement of one's values."
—Ayn Rand

*"Integrity: the greatest of all virtues...
with it, nothing else matters;
without it, nothing else matters."*

"The purpose of life is a life of purpose."
—Robert Byrne

Optimize Your Life!
Quick Results: Values

List the first values that come to mind, that are important to you.

Whereas I value. . .

3.1: VALUES—PERSONAL *CORE* VALUES

Review the "core" values and select those that are important to you. Then rank them 1 to 7, #1 being the most important. Explain *why* each is important and *how you express it*.

RANK:	Integrity - Why?
	Integrity - How?

RANK:	Honesty - Why?
	Honesty - How?

RANK:	Fidelity - Why?
	Fidelity - How?

RANK:	Courage - Why?
	Courage - How?

RANK:	Patience - Why?
	Patience - How?

RANK:	Justice - Why?
	Justice - How?

RANK:	Humility - Why?
	Humility - How?

3.2: VALUES—PERSONAL *INTERNAL* VALUES

Review the "internal" values and select those that are important to you. Rank them 1 to 7, #1 being the most important. Explain *why* each is important and *how you express it.*

RANK:	Humor - Why?
	Humor - How?
RANK:	Freedom - Why?
	Freedom - How?
RANK:	Opportunity - Why?
	Opportunity - How?
RANK:	Independence - Why?
	Independence - How?
RANK:	Challenge - Why?
	Challenge - How?
RANK:	Curiosity - Why?
	Curiosity - How?
RANK:	Other - Why?
	Other - How?

3.3: VALUES—PERSONAL *EXTERNAL* VALUES

Review the "external" values and select those that are important to you. Rank them 1 to 7, #1 being the most important. Explain *why* each is important and *how you express it.*

RANK:	Friendship - Why?	
	Friendship - How?	
RANK:	Sharing - Why?	
	Sharing - How?	
RANK:	Loyalty - Why?	
	Loyalty - How?	
RANK:	Acceptance - Why?	
	Acceptance - How?	
RANK:	Consideration - Why?	
	Consideration - How?	
RANK:	Love - Why?	
	Love - How?	
RANK:	Other - Why?	
	Other - How?	

Identify your personal Values Statement for your Life and your future.

Values Statement: Initial version

Values Statement: Follow-up version

Values Statement: Latest version

Is your statement: Clear - Concise - Meaningful - Easy to remember
Accurate - Dynamic - Powerful - Focused?

3.5: VALUES—PERSONAL VALUES CHECKLIST

For 7 days, enter the number of times per day you exhibit a particular value. Then add up how many days you exhibited the various values and observe which values are predominant in your everyday life. Keep track of which category of values you exhibit the most.
TIP: The Interactive Worksheets version of this calculates the totals for you!

Value	Day # 1	2	3	4	5	6	7	Total
Core Values								
Integrity								
Honesty								
Fidelity								
Courage								
Patience								
Justice								
Humility								
Total times exhibited Core Values:								
Internal Values								
Humor								
Freedom								
Opportunity								
Independence								
Challenge								
Curiosity								
Total times exhibited Internal Values:								
External Values								
Friendship								
Sharing								
Loyalty								
Acceptance								
Consideration								
Love								
Cooperation								
Total times exhibited External Values:								

Chapter 4

What Are You Doing Now?

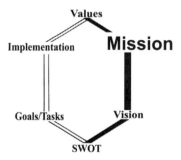

"A winner is someone who recognizes his God-given talents, works his tail off to develop them into skills, and uses these skills to accomplish his goals.
—Larry Bird

"No, I don't think our marriage would benefit from a mission statement."

Chapter 4
What Are You Doing Now?
Formulating a Personal Mission Statement

*"Seek not, my soul, the life of the immortals; but enjoy to
the full the resources that are within thy reach."*
—Pindar

What is a Mission Statement?
Your Values Statement looked at your past, and your Mission
Statement will look at your present life.

The key questions here include: "Who are you *currently,* what
are you doing, and why are you doing the things you do?" While
this concept seems simple and easy to complete, since it involves
only you in the here and now, the creation of a Mission Statement
may require re-visiting over time to discover deeper, secreted aspects of you and who you really are. The purpose of a classic
Mission Statement is to:
- Define who you are in terms of body, mind, and soul
- Identify your distinctive competencies
- Focus on what you are currently doing
- Define what resources you have and how they are allocated

There is a question in the Mission Statement for classic strategic
planning that asks why the organization exists. This *existential*
question may be offensive when applied to *personal* strategic
planning, so it is presented here as "What is your purpose in life?"

Body, Mind, and Soul
Body. Worksheet 4.1, "Who am I?—My Body" asks for a brief
inventory about *your body,* that is, what you were given geneti-
cally and how you have managed that gift so far. Everybody, even
glamorous models, movie stars, or Olympic athletes have likes
and dislikes about certain aspects of their body. In addition, society's views of the ideal body has changed over the ages and in

different parts of the world. Your goal now is to define your physical self. If you wish, you can also identify things you would like to change or improve. Later, you will create a plan to make the changes you select. The ultimate goal will be the reasonable improvement and, above all, the acceptance of your evolving body.

Mind. Use the same approach to complete an inventory of *your mind*—your mentality and your brains—using Worksheet 4.2, "Who Am I?—My Mind." Write a brief inventory of *what you know* (your formal and informal education) and what skills you have (what you can do with your education and experiences). Also look at how you use your mind, and how you keep it sharp and up-to-date, as well as how you can keep improving it. When asked why he started to study Greek at the age of 82, Ralph Waldo Emerson responded: "To improve my mind."

Soul. Worksheet 4.3, "Who Am I?—My Soul" addresses your soul, including your "psyche" (from Latin *psýchê*, from Greek *psukhê*, soul). This will be interesting and challenging, for it includes both your psychology and your spirituality. The latter deals with your views of and relationship with a Supreme Being, if you believe in one (or more than one, perhaps).

The Leadership Pyramid

The next step is to address your distinct competencies—those things you do well. One way of putting your competencies in perspective is by way of the author's concept of "The Leadership Pyramid."

While this concept was created for individuals in the world of business and professional life, it is also appropriate for your personal life—for, after all, you are the Leader of your life.

The base of this pyramid also starts with you and your *values*, your *persona*—the idealized image one wishes to present as distinguished from the *real* self—asking the question:

Who am I?

The next level addresses your formal and informal *education and*

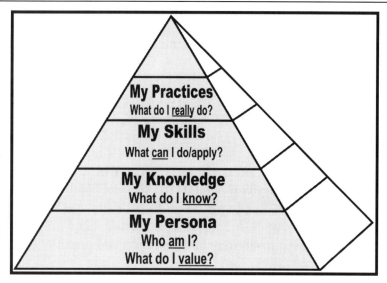

The Leadership Pyramid, © 1996 Bernhoff A. Dahl, M.D.

training, asking the question:

What do I know?

One starts with data, transforms it into useful information, reduces it into knowledge, and adapts and applies it to life, which results in wisdom.

Your knowledge, to be of any practical value, must be transformed, along with the input from *experience*, into applicable *skills*. This level asks:

What can I do/apply?

The next level addresses one's *practices* in real life; that is, it asks:

What do I really do?

This top level is more complex than might be assumed at first blush, for it includes such parameters as your risk tolerance, opportunity to act, challenges of the situation, and policies regarding risk and failure.

The apex of the pyramid is left blank here, for it may be labeled *Life* (to include all of one's life), *Goal* (to deal with a single defined Goal in one's life), *Job* (to address a specific employment opportunity), or *Task* (for dealing with a specific component of a larger project or goal). At the risk of trying to extract too much from this graphic, the apex could be labeled *Love, Sex, Money, Power,* etc.

In order for one to gain the apex, each of the levels must contribute all the necessary components for success. Each level has to be *in concert;* that is, lined up with all the other levels. The efforts must be in a timely fashion, for opportunity may only knock once. Otherwise the result may be frustration and possibly failure.

Distinct Competencies

To address the question of your competencies, you are referred to Worksheet 4.4, "Who Am I?—What Are Your Distinct Competencies?" A list of classic competencies is included in the Appendix as a prompt.

You will be surprised how many skills/competencies you have.

Spending Time

Worksheet 4.5, "Who Am I?—How Do I Spend My Time?" asks, "What are you currently doing?" While you could look at an "average" day, week, or month, it would probably be easier to see a year in your life and how you spend your time.

Emotions, Energy, and Money

One way of looking at your resources is by way of the simple acronym TEEM—Time, Energy, Emotions, and Money (including the things that money can buy). Since we have already addressed perhaps the most important resource—time—the last two worksheets in this chapter deal with your other key resources; namely, Worksheet 4.6, "Who Am I?—My Emotions and Energy," and Worksheet 4.7, "Who Am I?—My Financial Assets & Liabilities" which is a single page and may not provide space for all your data.

Purposes

Worksheet 4.8, "Who Am I?—What Is My Purpose In Life?" asks you to summarize what you feel is your main purpose in life, coupled with other purposes.

The Mission Statement

Finally, you'll create your personal Mission Statement using Worksheet 4.9, "Who Am I?—Creating My Mission Statement." You'll start with an initial version and revisit it later to update it. Refer to Worksheets 4.1 through 4.8 to see what you learned about yourself, and sum up the most important facets here.

Author's Suggestions

Values address your past; Mission your present. In the process of creating your Mission Statement, look deep inside yourself to your body, mind, and soul, as well as your formal and informal training, skills and competencies development, and your use of your resources (especially your time, energy, emotions, and money).

These challenges are best addressed by doing the easy stuff first, then revisiting and updating your statement as many times as you wish in the future. Do not get bogged down in too many details or negative issues, especially on your first pass through this material.

"We are not in a position in which we have nothing to work with. We already have capacities, talents, direction, missions, callings."
—Abraham Maslow

*"I have an existential map. It has
'You are here' written all over it."*
—Steven Wright

*"Do not dwell in the past,
do not dream of the future,
concentrate the mind on the present moment."*
—The Buddha

*"Mind what you have learned;
save you, it can."*
—Yoda, Jedi Master

Optimize Your Life!
Quick Results: Who Am I?/Mission

In light of my body, mind, and soul, as well as my
competencies, current activities, and resources...

My current activities include. . .

4.1: WHO AM I?—MY BODY

Summarize what your body is. You'll return later to rewrite it after you've learned more about yourself.

Initial version

I view my body as

Follow-up version

I view my body as

Latest version

I view my body as

4.2: WHO AM I?—MY MIND

Summarize what your mind is. You'll return later to rewrite it after you've learned more about yourself.

Initial version

I view my mind as

Follow-up version

I view my mind as

Latest version

I view my mind as

4.3: WHO AM I?—MY SOUL

Summarize what your soul (psyche and spirit) is. You'll return later to rewrite it after you've learned more about yourself.

Initial version

I view my soul (psyche and spirit) as

Follow-up version

I view my soul (psyche and spirit) as

Latest version

I view my soul (psyche and spirit) as

4.4: WHO AM I?—WHAT ARE MY DISTINCT COMPETENCIES?

List any skills you have learned, talents that are natural, or "gifts" you have been given in Life. Note how you learned them, who taught you, when you realized you had them, etc.

SKILL/TALENT/GIFT	ABOUT

4.5: WHO AM I?—HOW DO I SPEND MY TIME?

Rank how you spend your time, in order of importance.
Describe the activity.

RANK	ACTIVITY
	At work
	In education
	With spouse or intimate friend
	With family
	With close friends
	At play
	Other
	Other
	Other

4.6: WHO AM I?—MY EMOTIONS AND ENERGY

What people, forces, things...

1. ...make me happy

2. ...make me mellow

3. ...frustrate me

4. ...anger me

5. ...energize me

6. ...sap my energy

7. ...waste my time

8. Other

9. Other

10. Other

4.7: WHO AM I?—MY FINANCIAL ASSETS & LIABILITIES

Item	Cost/Valuation
Your primary residence (home or condominium) and other real estate	
Bank accounts, credit card data, and loan agreements	
Investments (stocks, bonds, mutual funds and CDs)	
Pension and other retirement accounts (IRA, 401(k), etc.)	
Insurance policies (life, home, and medical) and annuities	
Vehicles (cars, trucks, boats, airplanes, etc.)	
Social security data	
Buy-sell agreement(s) with business partners	
Jewelry and other personal property	
Your will and trust(s)	

4.8: WHO AM I?—WHAT IS MY PURPOSE IN LIFE?

Identify and define the purpose(s) of your Life.

MY MAIN PURPOSE IS:

MY OTHER PURPOSES ARE:

4.9: WHO AM I?—CREATING MY MISSION STATEMENT

Identify your personal Mission Statement. Define who you are in terms of mind, body, and soul; identify your competencies; focus on what you're currently do-ing; and define your resources.

Mission Statement: Initial version

Mission Statement: Follow-up version

Mission Statement: Latest version

Is your Statement Clear - Concise - Meaningful - Easy to remember - Accurate - Dynamic - Powerful - Focused?

"Some people see things that are and ask,
Why?
Some people dream of things
that never were and ask,
Why not?"
—George Bernard Shaw

Chapter 5

What Would You Like to Have/Do/Be in the Future?

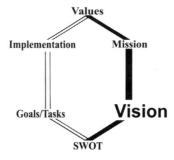

*"Cherish your visions and your dreams, as they are
the children of your soul; the blueprints of your
ultimate achievements."*
—Napoleon Hill

Henry began to question the connection between *visioning* **and swimming across the Atlantic Ocean.**

Chapter 5
What Would You Like to Have/Do/Be in the Future?
Envisioning a personal Vision Statement

"The soul never thinks without a picture."
—Aristotle

The Vision Statement answers the question:
*"What do you want to do, to have, to be, etc. in _____
(some point in the future)?"*

While your Values Statement looked at your past and the Mission Statement dealt primarily with the realities of the present with a view to the future, the Vision Statement is a dynamic collection of dreams and desires that addresses the *future*, usually at some specific time.

It is often convenient to group these visionary entities into short-term (less than one year), mid-term (1 to 5 years), and long-term (up to 10 years) time periods. There is also an interesting and compelling category that addresses the dreams and desires to complete "before you die."

Since the basic premise of *Optimize Your Life!* is that in order for you to optimize your life, you must take charge of it through planning and action, the question is raised:
"What future would you like to create?"

Visioning

The process you have been using has been one of collecting, categorizing, and defining data about you and your life's journey to date. The process has been one of convergence; that is, of narrowing and focusing.

The process of visioning, however, is one of divergence; that is, one of expanding one's personal database while looking to the future. Visioning is the powerful force that can help guide your life's journey into the future.

Visioning in *personal* strategic planning is:

- focused on you first, then on your relationship with your world
- an expedition from your past and present into your future
- a journey from the known into the unknown, from the tangible to the mystical
- a trip beyond the limits of numbers, assets, etc., but still rooted in reality
- an extension of your Mission Statement: your body/mind/soul as well as your competencies, resources, and purposes in life
- sensitive to your Values Statement: your core, internal, and external values
- a process that uses tools such as imagery, symbols, and stories
- a technique that employs "thinking outside the box"
- metaphorically, the top of the mountain you are now climbing
- your opportunity to dream the impossible dream
- the ultimate chance to "let it all hang out"
- your time to take charge of your destiny and create a better tomorrow
- your private excursion into your future: share it with others cautiously
- a bit scary and mysterious, but will energize, inspire, and motivate you into action
- the prelude to the definition and selection of specific and focused goals
- a process that focuses on your passion for life

The process of successful visioning employs a wide range of mental techniques from simple daydreaming to formal brainstorming, free association, and mind mapping. While mental games may be fun, mind-expanding, and creative, the visioning process must eventually be reduced to writing, for writing is concrete. Writing is not subject to the whims and distortions of human memory and machinations.

On Having or Being

In his 1976 book entitled *To Have or Be,* psychoanalyst Erich Fromm reflects on his life and previous writings as he questions society's values and makes some predictions. He focuses on two modes of existence of modern mankind.

The "having mode" is dedicated to material possessions and the necessary aggressiveness (including war) to gain those possessions. He notes that the success of an industrial society, based either on capitalism or communism, relies on increased production of material goods and the commitment by the population to purchase more and more.

The "being mode" is characterized by love, caring, and regard for humanity. He calls for a simple pattern of living wherein one is satisfied with some, but not excessive, possessions. Herein, a "Being" life focuses on giving, sharing, and sacrifice.

The ultimate visioning exercise is to re-organize the results of your visioning into the categories that address what you want to "have, do and be." This process moves one from the tangible aspects of life (*having* and *doing*) to the mystical (simply *being*). It may be a worthwhile exercise for you.

Aristotle Revisited

In Chapter 3, the moral (or social) ethics of Aristotle were introduced in a simple table form, along with lists of so-called core values, internal values, and external values. They were included to assist the reader in addressing the possible factors that may play a role in the assessment of their own values. The lists of values did not include definitions, since they were all in common modern use and so that your completion of the worksheets could be efficient and unencumbered by formal definitions. Since the terms used in the Aristotelian ethics came from ancient Greek, to Latin, and then on to the Germanic languages including English, these terms need to be defined and explored in greater detail.

In this chapter on visioning, looking to the future, we will revisit Aristotle's virtues and vices since it is an ideal time for the reader to evaluate their own virtues and then to incorporate them in the divergent list of possible foci of emphasis for action in their future. Visioning is a time to be all-inclusive, to include all possibilities to have, to do, and to be. Subsequently we will prioritize and select a limited number of specific goals—a convergent process.

This book draws upon the world of philosophy (from Greek *philos,* "love of" and *sophos,* "wisdom") as defined in its broadest sense—that is the historical basis for all human knowledge. Philosophy can be defined as the critical search for unconditioned knowledge based on rational thinking (from Greek *logos,* "logic, reason") and not from myth or so-called divine inspiration. Philosophy uses the power of questions as the key form of inquiry.

The key philosophical questions can be grouped into three major areas:

1. **Knowledge:** What exists? (The study of ontology) What is known? (The study of epistemology)
2. **Conduct:** How should we behave? (The study of ethics)
3. **Governance:** How should we interact in society? (The study of politics)

Aristotle was born in 385 B.C. in the coastal town of Stragira in Macedonia, the son of a court physician to King Amyntas of Macedonia. Early in life he showed an interest in the study of nature and living things and at the age of seventeen was sent to Athens to study at Plato's Academy where he stayed for twenty years—first as a student, and later a teacher.

The Greek philosophers of Aristotle's time stood on the shoulders of writers and thinkers of the previous 500 years, drawing from the wisdom and accomplishments from ancient India, Egypt, Assyria, Persia, and Babylonia. In the ancient Greek world first there were the natural physiologists (from Greek *phusis,* "nature" and *logos,* "logic, reason") such as Thales, Heraclitus, and Parmenides who struggled with the origin of the cosmos (of Being or Becoming). They were the first to go beyond myths or stories and tried to understand the world by way of the rational thinking processes. There was Pythagoras who worshiped numbers and set out to explain the cosmos from a mathematical perspective. Then came the Sophists, who went from looking at the universe to focusing on humans and not just nature. They were traveling tutors who taught rhetoric, the art of speaking well, of persuasion. Chief among them was Protagoras, best known for his statement:

"Man is the measure of all things, of those that are that they are, and of those that are not that they are not."

This is interpreted as there is nothing that is good or bad unto itself; everything is relative to the situation. Above all, everything is relative to the power of rhetoric; that is, the strongest argument wins.

Along came Socrates, who took exception to the relativists and became an outspoken proponent of absolute truths. He was an unattractive and unkempt philosopher who walked the streets of Athens engaging people in dialogues, discussions, and even arguments between two parties. He asked tough questions and maneuvered his opponents into embarrassing logical situations. Eventually the authorities put him on trial, convicted him of "corrupting the youth of Athens" and forced him to commit suicide by way of "taking the hemlock."

Next came Plato, who although not a student of Socrates (for Socrates did not teach in the conventional sense of the times), gathered information about Socrates' dialogues, added much of his own wisdom, organized the Academy to teach young philosophers, and was a prolific writer.

As a student of Plato, and later a teacher at The Academy, Aristotle studied, organized bodies of knowledge, and was also a prolific writer. Among his writings were poems, dialogues, a major book on nature (physics from the Greek *phusis,* "nature"), and a second book on the logical study of reality (*Metaphysics,* which means "a book written after *Physics*"), as well *Nicomachean Ethics,* a collection of ten books, each divided into chapters.

In the *Nicomachean Ethics* Aristotle defines the final goal (Greek *telos,* "end") of mankind is happiness. The term he used for happiness in Greek was *eudemonia,* which reflects more than just an emotion but rather excellence or success in life. The Greek culture at the time of Aristotle was focused on excellence (or in Greek, *aristhea*). While there are many things mankind desires in life, like money or power, or pure pleasure, these are just *means* (or avenues) to attain the final goal—the end goal of true eudemonia, which Aristotle describes as *the* function of mankind. Happiness is not a state of mind but an activity, an on-going process, not merely pleasure.

Aristotle defines ethics simply as doing what is good for mankind. As a scientist, he was drawn to the process of observations, that is, using the method of empiricism (from Greek *empeiros,* "skilled"), the basis for the scientific method. The scientific method includes five steps:

1. Stating the problem
2. Forming the hypothesis
3. Observing the experiment
4. Interpreting the data
5. Drawing the conclusion

He went about the community of Athens and beyond and studied the behavior, emotions, and attitudes of a diverse group of successful and powerful men in Athens. After gathering his data, he collated and organized it in such a way as to make conclusions as a scientist.

The term virtue that we use today comes from the Latin word *virtus* ("manliness, excellence, goodness"), while the original term in Greek used by Aristotle is *aristea.* Virtue can considered a good state of the soul or psyche (from Greek *psuche*), as health is a good state of the body. Aristotle concluded that the proper practice of virtues was the only avenue to reaching eudemonia.

How does one obtain virtues? Virtues are not naturally attained through genetics, but rather are learned during life, and practiced to perfection like any other skill. Perfected and practiced enough and they may become habits...good habits.

Let us now address the moral (social) virtues, which will require a bit of struggle to understand the words which have been translated over the centuries from ancient Greek to modern English. The use of synonyms may help to bridge that etymological gap. Most scholarly lists include the following twelve virtues along with their vices; that is, the states of excess or lack of a virtue.

1. **Courage** as a virtue is defined as the feelings of fear or confidence in the face of danger, external threats. The emotional response may lead to action. The vices are cowardice at one end and recklessness at the other.

2. **Temperance** is a virtue that deals with our response to the pleasures and pain of bodily functions namely food, drink, and sex. While the virtue of temperance calls for a life of moderation, the vice of excess is self-indulgence and the lack is insensitivity.

3. **Liberality** is a virtue which addresses the issue of managing and sharing one's money of a person of modest assets. The vice of failing to properly share one's riches is labeled as wastefulness; at the opposite pole is miserliness.

4. **Magnificence** is a virtue that relates to liberality and applies to the person of great riches and their appropriate giving and sharing with their community. Magnificence is the "golden mean" between the vice of excessive giving, vulgarity or tastelessness, and pettiness associated with minimal giving.

5. **Magnanimity** is the virtue that deals with the major aspects of one's honor and dishonor, their standing, in their community. An excess is vanity; the lack, timidity.

6. **Pride/Proper Ambition** is a virtue that relates to magnanimity but at a lesser level. It has also been labeled industriousness. The vice of excess is overzealousness; that of lack, procrastination or undue humility.

7. **Patience/Good temper** is the virtue of successfully dealing with the complex passion of anger, an emotion, a feeling that one does not choose but one that must be dealt with. Aristotle notes that there are many circumstances in which anger is appropriate. The vice of excessive response to an-

ger is impatience and at the opposite pole the "lack of spirit" or acquiescence.

8. **Truthfulness** is the virtue that does not focus on honesty and lying, as the reader might expect, but on the concept of being "true to oneself," knowing oneself and one's self expression. The vice of excess is boastfulness, while the lack has been called false modesty.

9. **Wittiness** is the virtue of proper humor in conversation while the extremes are silliness and rudeness.

10. **Friendliness** is a virtue of major importance to Aristotle for he spends two of the ten books of the *Nicomachean Ethics* on this vital subject. He focuses on the importance of having friends, for true happiness requires friends. It is, however, important that friends share the same virtues, for together they can develop, apply, and improve one's virtues over time. The excess of friendliness is servility; the deficiency, unfriendliness.

11. **Modesty** is the virtue that addresses the issue of an appropriate sense of shame as compared to the excessive vice of shyness or the deficient state of the vice of shamelessness.

12. **Righteous indignation** is the virtue of emotions being aroused by something that is unjust. The vices of envy and spitefulness are at the extremes of excess and efficiency, respectively.

Intellectual Virtues

In addition to these twelve social virtues, Aristotle offers insights about a wide range of intellectual virtues, such as knowledge about science (the habit of logical reasoning), art (from Greek *techne,* "the habit of knowing how to build things"), and intuition (from Greek *nous,* "the habit of insight and opening the mind"). However, the most intriguing intellectual virtue is prudence

Prudence

Prudence is the virtue of practical wisdom, perhaps just common sense, or even "street smarts." It is the habit of how to act in human life, how to pull together and apply the other virtues so as to gain the goals of life. It is the true "golden mean" in any situation wherein a virtue or several virtues will be called upon, in a timely fashion without undue hesitation, to act, to succeed, to gain eudemonia, true happiness.

The Cardinal Virtues

Aristotle, and Plato before him, focused on four key virtues that later became known as the Cardinal Virtues, from the Latin word *cardin-,* meaning "hinge," for they were hinged on the door of a virtuous life. The Cardinal Virtues were adapted by St. Augustine and later Thomas Aquinas and are included in the Christian church along with faith, hope, and charity to create the Heavenly Virtues or the Seven Cardinal Virtues.

The Cardinal Virtues include three virtues that we have covered—namely, courage, temperance, and prudence. The fourth virtue is justice for which Aristotle assigned a complete book. While much of his writings on justice cover the judicial or legal system of a city state, some aspects of his writing can be readily and practically applied to individuals in their search for happiness. The first is *corrective justice,* which is based on an arithmetic model wherein exact quantities of goods or services are given in exchange on a voluntary or involuntary basis, regardless of a person's status. The second is *distributive justice,* that is the virtue based on a geometric model wherein the distribution is relevant to such issues as a person's ability, need, or risk.

There are, of course, many actions that simply go beyond right and wrong, wherein they are pure vice with no possible virtue, such as adultery, thievery, and murder.

Virtues in Summary

One could describe a virtue as the ability of approaching a situation with confidence, employing a learned and perfected habit, eliciting an appropriate emotional response, making the right decision, and leading to the right action at the right time.

Properly employed, a virtue may lead to pleasure or success, even in extremely hostile environments.

As to the goals for a successful life, Aristotle suggested that it be a long enough life with reasonable health, with adequate material prosperity, with close and virtuous friends and family, and ending with honor and respect in the view of one's community.

In this chapter on visioning, it is interesting to note that in Aristotle's world of the scientific method, the Greek term *theoria* means "visioning the future." Herein, we are developing the theory of *your* future.

A Look at Desires

Although this book is based on the driving power of values in all our lives (Chapter 3), there is another approach to addressing the factors that motivate you—namely, desires. As you have seen in our visioning process, your dreams and desires must be in concert with your values for successful strategic planning.

Psychologist Steven Reiss, Ph.D., recently published a book entitled *Who Am I? The 16 Desires That Motivate Our Actions and Define Our Personalities* (see Bibliography). He reviewed the literature regarding the theories of motivation and collected more than 400 goals that reflect what important motivators in the lives of humans are, and pared them down to sixteen basic desires. In his book, Dr. Reiss discusses the sixteen desires in detail and addressed their specific applications to individuals and their relationships. In his chapter entitled *Values-Based Happiness,* he noted that even if a well-selected goal is not completed, the act alone can make a life meaningful and satisfying.

Aristotelian View of Virtuous People

In Worksheet 5.4, you are encouraged to enter the names of current or historical people from throughout the world who you hold in high regard as to their expressed virtues. On Worksheet 2.3, we addressed "influential people in your life"; but this Worksheet asks you to look beyond your own world—to people you most likely do not know on a personal level.

The Visioning Process: Your Current World

To carry out the formal aspects of visioning, find a quiet place at a time when you are well-rested, nourished, and have little likelihood of being interrupted. You may wish to have music playing quietly in the background. While a little wine may facilitate visioning, too much alcohol will undermine the process. The fumes of marijuana or the use of other recreational drugs are certainly detrimental. While an LSD flashback might be interesting, it would destroy all attempts at rational visioning.

Above all, do your personal visioning alone.

Start the visioning process by getting 10 to 20 large sheets of paper (ideally, flip-chart size) and a handful of sharp pencils—or, better yet, a collection of felt-tipped pens in a range of your favorite colors. You may wish to use large flip-chart-sized Post-Its, so you can write on them and then stick them to the wall. You will be able to see all of your work at one glance, relate one sheet to another, and merge the data easily.

Next, review the worksheets from your endeavors to date. These are the Personal Inventory Worksheets in Chapter 2, the Values Worksheets in Chapter 3, and the Mission Worksheets in Chapter 4. To facilitate the process of visioning, it is usually best to start with mid-term goals; that is, goals that should be completed successfully in up to five years. You will soon realize that many of your life's goals will cover a span of time well beyond five years. Some must be done as soon as possible.

Review this data from previous chapters, then start to make a list of all the things that are *positive* in your current life on the right side of this Current Data Sheet. This can be as long a list as you wish. List everything that gives you pleasure, that gives you a "feel good" response. List everything that makes you proud of yourself. Look first at your body, mind, and soul, then into your resources and your world. Consider relationships with family, friends, education, career, society in general, and God. Simply put, look on the brighter side of life.

On the left side of the Current Data Sheet, using the most dramatic colored pen you have, make a list of the *negatives* in your life. Consider the same areas or categories as mentioned above. Next to each of these negative or "toxic" aspects of your life, write down some ideas of how you might most effectively eliminate or reduce their impact on your life. While this addresses your future life, you can take advantage of the emotional charge as you list these items.

By now you have a collection of related and unrelated words and ideas. The next step is to group these entities based on their commonality, both the positive and the negative.

The Visioning Process: Your Future World
The next step is to create and title separate Facet of Life Sheets, one for each of the major facets of your life. While there are many potential facets in anyone's life, some of the most common include:

1. Intimate relationships
2. Family
3. Friends and society
4. Education
5. Career
6. Finances
7. Recreation and travels
8. Specific body/mind/soul issue

Addressing each of the positive or negative items on the Current Data Sheet, select and copy to any appropriate Facet of Life Sheets. You will notice that some of these items may be entered on more than one Facet of Life Sheet.

The next step is to review the results of your entries on Worksheets 5.1, 5.2, and 5.3, and enter selected desires, wishes, and dreams onto their appropriate Facet of Life Sheet. Next to each of the desires, wishes, or dreams entered on the Facets of Life Sheets, write down necessary actions needed to attain them.

While these instructions only constitute several sentences, the process of selecting and entering these items may take time, energy, and emotions and may need to be revisited later.

During this process, list as many dreams, wishes, and end results you can imagine, even beyond those you already entered into Worksheets 5.1, 5.2, and 5.3. The visioning process seeks quantity, not quality. Quantity will breed quality in the next step (Chapter 6) where you will formulate and prioritize well-defined and specific goals. This process of maximizing the number of dreams, desires, and end results for your life and narrowing them down to a manageable number is like tapping a Vermont sugar maple and boiling the sap down (33:1) to syrup. In the upcoming Goals process, you will reduce the maple syrup to candy.

Eventually you will be satisfied that you have put on paper all of your dreams and desires as well as the accompanying actions necessary to bring them to fruition. Then merge as many as possible that have commonality. You will probably end up with anywhere from thirty to fifty... even a hundred desirable end results for the next five years of your life. Some may appear to be easily attainable, some very difficult, some even unlikely.

Keep them all!

The Vision Statement

Finally, create your personal Vision Statement using Worksheet 5.5, "Creating My Vision Statement." At this point, review your Values and Mission Statements to ensure they are *in concert* with your Vision Statement. Start with an initial version and revisit it later to update.

Examples of Vision Statements

"I have a dream..."
—Martin Luther King

*"There is nothing like
a dream to create
the future."*
—Victor Hugo

"We choose to go to the moon..."
—John F. Kennedy

"If you can dream it, you can do it."
—Walt Disney

Author's Suggestions

The process of visioning your future is exciting and invigorating. It may also be intimidating, for we all share some fear about the future, especially death. The process calls for looking back and then forward as we define our bridge to the future. While only a few of us have a truly "clean slate" in life, the visioning process encourages us to take a fresh view of our lives and to push the envelope of dreams and desires.

Although you live in the world with others, your dreams are private; so you need to take this journey into your future alone. As in ancient and mythical times, you too, must travel alone on your personal quest. Using the power of *Optimize Your Life!*, you may wish to take an even deeper journey, the Journey into the Self. For that Quest, you may welcome or need a trusted friend or professional to assist you.

The current literature and concepts for successful leadership list the role of the leader's vision as key. Since you are the leader of your life, your vision is of utmost importance to you. Develop it well.

"Champions aren't made in gyms.
Champions are made from something
they have deep inside them:
a desire, a dream, a vision."
—Muhammad Ali

"It is preoccupation with possessions, more than
anything else, that prevents us from living
freely and nobly."
—Bertrand Russell

"He who possesses most must be most afraid of loss."
—Leonardo da Vinci

"Go confidently in the direction of your dreams.
Live the life you imagined."
—Henry David Thoreau

"We are confronted with insurmountable opportunities."
—Walt Kelly, *Pogo*

Optimize Your Life!
Quick Results: Vision

Based on my values and mission...

In the near future, I would like to have/be/do. . .

5.1: WHAT DO I WANT TO *HAVE...*

Identify what you want to have—categorized as *short-term* (this year), *mid-term* (1-5 years), and *long-term* (up to 10 years).

...this year? (Short-term)

...in the next 1-5 years? (Mid-term)

...up to 10 years? (Long-term)

5.2: WHAT DO I WANT TO *DO...*

Identify what you want to do—categorized as *short-term* (this year), *mid-term* (1-5 years), and *long-term* (up to 10 years).

...this year? (Short-term)

...in the next 1-5 years? (Mid-term)

...up to 10 years? (Long-term)

5.3: WHAT DO I WANT TO *BE...*

Identify what you want to be—categorized as *short-term* (this year), *mid-term* (1-5 years), and *long-term* (up to 10 years).

...this year? (Short-term)

...in the next 1-5 years? (Mid-term)

...up to 10 years? (Long-term)

5.4: ARISTOTELIAN VIEW OF VIRTUOUS PEOPLE

What individuals you do not know personally but have respect and admiration for their virtues? Fill in names and, when you're finished, rank them in order of importance—consider the virtues most important to you, and the individual's effect on you, with "1" being the most important. You may wish to revisit pages 44 and 79-82 to review virtues.

RANK	PERSON	NOTABLE VIRTUES

5.5: CREATING MY VISION STATEMENT

Identify your personal Vision Statement for your Life and your future.

Vision Statement: Initial version

Vision Statement: Follow-up version

Vision Statement: Latest version

Is your Statement Clear - Concise - Meaningful - Easy to remember
Accurate - Dynamic - Powerful - Focused?

Chapter 6

What Is Your
SCOT Analysis?

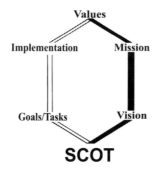

SCOT

*"Opportunity is missed by most people
because it is dressed in overalls
and looks like work."*
—Thomas Edison

Chapter 6
What Is Your SCOT Analysis?
Identifying your Strengths, Challenges,
Opportunities, and Threats

*"Make it thy business to know thyself, which is the
most difficult lesson in the world."*
—Miguel de Cervantes

The next step in classic organizational strategic planning is the
so-called SWOT analysis, an acronym that addresses the organization's *internal* **strengths** and **weaknesses**, as well as its *external* **opportunities** and **threats.** This analysis looks first inside
and then outside the organization, into the world in which the organization exists. This process has also been labeled the *performance audit* and *environmental scan.*

Challenges vs. Weaknesses
Most classic *organizational* strategic planning programs talk
about "SWOT"—Strengths, Weaknesses, Opportunities, and
Threats. The *Optimize Your Life!* approach prefers the term
"SCOT"—where "Challenges" replace "Weaknesses." One's
limitations or shortcomings need not be viewed as negative; they
are merely obstacles that challenge us to "think outside the box"
and improve ourselves.

The formation of your Values Statement addressed your *past;*
your Mission Statement focused on your *present;* and the Vision
Statement created your vision of your *future.* Throughout the
process, you collected and sorted out a great deal of material:
ideas, concepts, facts, thoughts, etc., which can now be applied to
the formulation of your SCOT analysis. This is a prelude to defining and selecting your specific Goals.

Strengths and Challenges Analysis
In addressing an *organization's* Strengths and Challenges, the

process first defines a series of categories and then formulates thought-provoking questions in each category. The categories selected would be directly related to the mission of the organization, and may include generic categories such as: history and reputation, past successes and failures, leadership, ownership, governance, reward systems, technology, management practices, human resources (personnel), facilities and space, equipment, location, financial status, risk aversion or tolerance, and current and past strategic planning. While these categories have proved successful for organizational strategic planning and several may be inappropriate for *personal* planning, they do offer a stimulus for a range of possibilities.

In addressing one's personal strengths there are a range of categories for one's *body, mind,* and *soul* that can stimulate key questions: What are your:

- Positive aspects regarding your body?
- Talents or gifts you were given (genetic)?
- Skills and competencies you have acquired?
- Expressions of a positive attitude and humor?
- Practices regarding proper risk management?
- Resources such as finances and material assets?
- Reputation and past successes?
- Relationships with individuals and organizations?
- Attitudes about spirituality?
- Positive habits?

Strengths. On Worksheets 6.1, "SCOT Analysis: My Strengths" and 6.2, "SCOT Analysis: My Strengths: Body, Mind, & Soul," you can answer the generic questions and add others that address your strengths. There is also an opportunity to address the past successful use of your strengths as well as their uses in the future.

Challenges. Addressing your challenges may be a daunting task. It calls for the discipline of pure introspection and personal honesty. We all have foibles, shortcomings, and faults. Some can be minimized, some even completely corrected—if we are willing to try, on our own or with the help of benevolent individuals or professionals. The same categories, given above for addressing your Strengths, usually stimulate thoughts, questions, and answers about your personal challenges.

Worksheets 6.3, "SCOT Analysis: My Challenges," and 6.4, "SCOT Analysis: My Challenges: Body, Mind & Soul," deal with your challenges and offer an opportunity to address their diminution or correction.

Opportunities and Threats Analysis

During the SCOT analysis process, often an external threat may, on closer examination, be viewed as an opportunity. It is interesting to note that the Chinese pictograph for "crisis" is the combined pictographs of "threat" *and* "opportunity."

An organization must address its *external* world, gauging its

 **Crisis = Threat + Opportunity**

opportunities and threats to acquire accurate information and facts. These are often difficult to obtain, trust, analyze, and incorporate (synthesize) into a strategic plan. A strategic planning facilitator may proceed by defining certain categories, such as: the economy (local, regional, national, worldwide); competitors and contemporaries; government intervention; demographics; market-*share* and market*place*; clients, customers, and suppliers; and organizational mergers, acquisitions, consolidations, and alliances.

Again, in adapting to an individual's personal strategic planning, many of these categories can be applied, even though, on an initial scan, they may seem inappropriate. The goal is to discover how you perceive your world and how you gain and process data about it.

On a personal level, you can address categories that stimulate questions such as determining what your opportunities are. These may include:

- Optimal use of your body and physical capabilities
- Proper use of your mind, skills, and competencies
- Application of your spirituality
- Appropriate use of your formal and informal education
- Utilization of your practical skills
- Seeking and maintaining satisfying employment or professional life
- Intimate relationship and a quality family life
- Friendship and a satisfying social life
- Avoidance or diminution of toxic forces and people
- Economic and political trends

Opportunities. Worksheet 6.5, "SCOT Analysis: Opportunities," and 6.6, "SCOT Analysis: Opportunities: Body, Mind, & Soul," are designed to address these questions. Enter specific responses to be used next in defining and selecting specific goals.

Threats. Look at the threats from your outside world. You can use the same categories and questions, but first look at the downside—the negative aspects that may be present or looming in the near future. Worksheet 6.7, "SCOT Analysis: Threats," will assist you in focusing on threats.

Author's Suggestions

At this point, you're covering material you've dealt with before. You are asked to address different questions that may well end up with the same answers. This process, albeit duplicative, can build on your previous responses and yield new information as you dig deeper into yourself and your world.

The big challenge of the opportunities and threats phase for organizations is the difficulty in gaining and analyzing reliable information about the current and possible future external environment. The data sources may be as varied as newspapers and magazines, web sites, consultants, seminars and workshops, rumor, network resources, site visits (so-called *scouting*), and commercial databases. The attendees during strategic planning will be forced outside of the "comfort zone" of their personal knowledge and organizational database and into the future world of change and chaos, the unknown and the feared. The same is true of the practitioner of personal strategic planning.

During a free-flowing SCOT analysis, the database expands and there is a concomitant link between the external opportunities and threats and the internal strengths and weaknesses. This process of expansion and linkage usually generates a whole host of specific ideas that can augment the visioning process by formulating additional, specific goals.

On Seeking Your Comfort Zone:

"The data you have is not what you want.
The data you want is not what you need.
The data you need is not available."
—Finagle's Law

"Info, info everywhere,
but no one stops to think."
—H. Krantzberg

"Everyone has talent.
What is rare is the courage to
follow it to the dark places
where it can lead."
—Erica Jong

Optimize Your Life!
Quick Results: SC Analysis

List your **strengths** and **challenges** that first come to mind.

Optimize Your Life!
Quick Results: OT Analysis

List your **opportunities** and **threats** that first come to mind.

6.1: SCOT ANALYSIS: MY STRENGTHS

Identify *internal* Strengths

What are my greatest *given* Strengths (gifts, talents)?

What gifts/talents have I failed to develop or use?

What are my greatest *acquired* Strengths (my applied skills)?

Which skills have I failed to use optimally?

What do people who know me well view as my Strengths?

6.2: SCOT ANALYSIS: MY STRENGTHS: Body, Mind, & Soul

Identify the Strengths of your body, mind, and soul.

What are the Strengths of *my body?*

What are the Strengths of *my mind?*

What are the Strengths of *my soul?*

What are my *good habits?*

Other:

6.3: SCOT ANALYSIS: MY CHALLENGES

Identify *internal* Challenges

What are my greatest personal Challenges?

What can/will I do now to diminish or correct each one?

What do people who know me well view as my Challenges?

What are my fears and obsessions?

What do I do in excess that is destructive?

6.4: SCOT ANALYSIS: MY CHALLENGES: Body, Mind, & Soul

Identify the Challenges of your body, mind, and soul

What are the Challenges of *my body* and how can I correct them?

What are the Challenges of *my mind* and how can I correct them?

What are the Challenges of *my soul* and how can I correct them?

What are my *bad habits,* and how can I change them?

Other:

6.5: SCOT ANALYSIS: OPPORTUNITIES

What optimal employment/education Opportunities are available?

What intimate relationships/family life are obtainable?

What friendships/social life are attainable?

Other:

Other:

6.6: SCOT ANALYSIS: OPPORTUNITIES: Body, Mind, & Soul

Identify Opportunities of your body, mind, and soul

How can I best use the Strengths of *my body?*

How can I best use the Strengths of *my mind?*

How can I best use the Strengths of *my soul?*

Other:

Other:

6.7: SCOT ANALYSIS: THREATS

Identify Threats

What, in my life, do I need to get rid of?

What economic problems do I need to address?

What relationship issues do I need to resolve?

Other:

Other:

"The reason most people never reach their goals is that they don't define them, or ever seriously consider them as believable or achievable.

Winners can tell you where they are going, what they plan to do along the way, and who will be sharing the adventure with them."

—Denis Waitley

Chapter 7

What Are Your Goals?

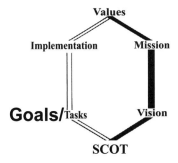

"I destabilized when I should have prioritized."

Chapter 7
What Are Your Goals?
Selecting your specific goals

"Man is a goal-seeking animal. His life only has meaning
if he is reaching out and striving for his goals."
—Aristotle

What Is A Goal?

A Goal is a well-defined target, an end point that focuses energy and effort from the past and present, to take you into the future. A Goal may be exceedingly practical when focused on a revenue-producing career, or it may be a laudable dream when an amateur author aims to write a bestselling book.

A carefully chosen Goal draws from the *past* when you evaluate the power of your values and create your Values Statement. It includes the *present* when you consider the many aspects of your mission and develop your Mission Statement. A Goal also incorporates your vision of your *future;* that is, your choices of the things you would like to have, to do, and to be in the near or distant future. Included in a well-crafted Goal are key components from your SCOT analysis. The major factors involved in the dynamics of generating a rational Goal with a high degree of successful implementation is represented by the Goals graphic.

Identifying Goals

While Goal-setting is related to all the factors mentioned above, the visioning process (in Chapter 5) is the most important prelude to identifying Goals. Unlike visioning, which is divergent, Goal-setting is convergent; that is, a process of selecting and prioritizing.

There are many sources of efforts, emotions, and energy that must be tapped in defining a Goal and considerably more energy in implementing it. A properly chosen and executed Goal will not only focus all this energy but also magnify and maximize the energy that emerges from this successful strategic plan and its execution. This process is *synergistic:* the results exceed the sum of the input, in which 2 plus 2 is greater than 4.

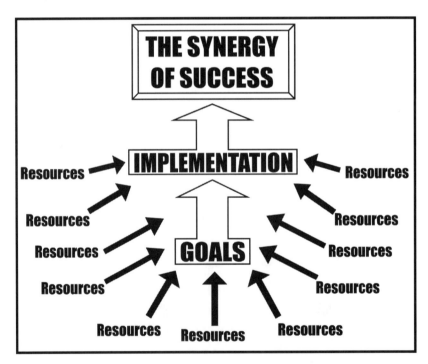

Maslow's Hierarchy of Needs

The selection of a potential Goal usually starts in the body of the Vision Statement, in which the wishes and wants for the future are defined. A review of your personal Vision Statement from Chapter 5 will provide this initial step.

At this point it might be wise to take a step back and look at the work of the humanistic psychologist Abraham Maslow, who in 1954 published *The Hierarchy of Needs*, represented by the graphic below.

Maslow's basic premise is that a person's motivation and resultant behavior are determined by his *needs*. He departed from others in his field who held that people are controlled by mechanical forces (stimuli and reinforcement of behaviors) or by unconscious instinctual forces favored by the various schools of psychoanalysis.

Maslow felt most people first meet the needs of the lowest level, that is *physiological or body needs* (such as needs for oxygen, water, food, and maintenance of body), lest they die. One can live without air for only minutes, without water for only a few days, and without food for up to forty days. A person can die

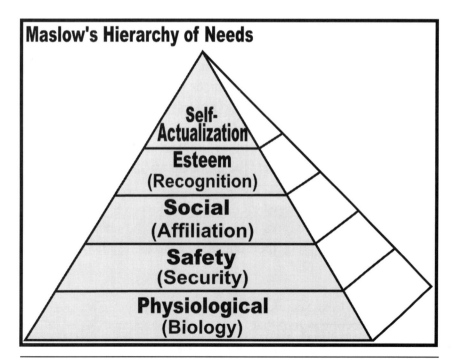

Maslow's Hierarchy of Needs

Self-Actualization
Esteem (Recognition)
Social (Affiliation)
Safety (Security)
Physiological (Biology)

from hypothermia in as little as ten minutes.

The second level, which addresses *safety and security needs,* focuses on the efforts to secure and maintain a stable environment with adequate shelter. It also includes planning for meeting the ongoing needs for level one and two. These first two levels are especially important for children to feel secure. However, adults' behaviors and motivations are rapidly modified to address these basic needs during times of war, riots, environmental disasters, and famine.

Level three, labeled *social or affiliation needs,* deals with a person's relationships with others, including family and friends as well as the larger outside world. There are three types of love as defined by the ancient Greeks: *agape* (divine love), *eros* (physical love), and *phileo* (friendship). In its broadest sense, efforts expended at this level are to meet the need to have a sense of belonging.

The fourth level, *esteem or recognition needs,* addresses a person's sense of self-respect, as well as respect from others in his world, so he can feel satisfied with his life performance.

The apex of Maslow's pyramid is *self-actualization,* wherein a person may reach beyond his personal life and respond to a "calling." Since this level is the least tangible or definable of the five levels of the hierarchy, it includes aspects of a mystical life. The calling may lure a person into a quest in the world of art, music, writing, or spirituality. While most people who reach this level have expended the efforts or enjoyed the luxury of having the four "lower" levels met, there are many striking exceptions, especially in the world of religion.

The Christian mystics of the first millennium, Hindu holy men, and many Buddhist monks have transcended the concerns of the first three levels to focus their entire lives on the top two.

S.M.A.R.T.

In the practical search for goals, the acronym SMART can stand for selecting a goal that is:

S = Specific (Is it specific and definable?)
M = Measurable (Can it be measured?)
A = Achievable (Can it be done?)
R = Realistic (Do you have the resources?)
T = Timely (Can it be done in time?)

In the creation and prioritization of a goal, one would be wise to ask if the goal is "smart."

On "Toxic" Forces and People

The history of mankind has been replete with despots, tyrants, and dictators. All of us find toxic or destructive people in our lives, some of whom may have power over us. It is also true that each of us has, within ourselves, some toxic aspects.

Some of these toxic behaviors come in the form of bad habits such as whining, procrastinating, defeatism, or being envious. Others are considerably more destructive, such as addiction, dishonesty, physical or psychological abuse, or thievery. Create your own list and review the list of Aristotle's Vices and Virtues in Chapter 3. Then decide what personality traits or behaviors are toxic, either in others or within you, that you can reduce, eliminate, or even accept.

Only you can decide what you will tolerate.

The Role of Time

The last factor, time, is often the major factor in the wise creation and selection of Goals. Decide when a Goal should be started and completed. There are short-term Goals that need to be addressed as soon as possible; you may need to respond to an immediate crisis or an opportunity. Next, there are the mid-term Goals that may have to be started within a year or as late as five years.

Last, there are longer-term Goals that may be started within ten years or longer. The time in which any specific Goal should be completed is a function of the complexity and nature of the Goal. Some Goals must be completed within an ordered sequence, and others may never be finished, even in a lifetime. As to lifetime

Goals, consider: *What do you want to do before you die?*

Goal Planning

The worksheets to assist you in goal selection and prioritization are 7.1, "Goals: Ultra-Short-Term Goals," 7.2, "Goals: Short-Term (this year)," 7.3, "Goals: Mid-Term (up to 5 years)," 7.4, "Goals: Long-Term (up to 10 years)," and 7.5, "Goals: Before You Die."

Start by reviewing your Vision Statement and the "Have, Do and Be" worksheets in Chapter 5. Using these worksheets, select and define potential Goals by merging "wants" from these four sources into definable Goals. Next, evaluate these Goals in light of the major factors indicated in the first graphic in this chapter. Ask the "SMART" questions that address the specificity, measurability, achievability, resource availability, and timeliness. Also revisit your Values Statement to ensure that a potential Goal is *in concert* with your values.

Worksheets 7.6, "Goals Matrix: You," and 7.7, "Goals Matrix: Your World," provide a place to collect your selected Goals.

Author's Suggestions

Selecting and prioritizing a limited number of specific and defined Goals is as important as it is demanding. These selections must match your available time and resources (which may change in the future).

"People are not lazy. They simply have impotent goals—
that is, goals that do not inspire them."
—Anthony Robbins

"Make your work to be in keeping with your goals."
—Leonardo da Vinci

"Whatever thy hand findest to do, do it with all thy heart."
—Jesus of Nazareth

"You must have long-term goals to keep from being frustrated by the short-term failures."
—Charles C. Noble

"You need to overcome the tug of people against you as you reach for high goals."
—General George S. Patton

"Our plans miscarry because they have no goal. When a man does not know what harbor he is making for, no wind is the right wind."
—Seneca

"Dreams are maps. We make the world significant by the courage of our questions and the depths of our answers."
—Carl Sagan

Optimize Your Life!
Quick Results: <u>Goals</u>

List three specific **goals** you can finish in the very near future.

1.
2.
3.

Goals-driven Ideas for an Optimized Life

Your **BODY**

1. **Safety**: always live defensively, yet stay positive.
2. **Nutrition**: eat adequate food and vitamins.
3. **Physical exercise**: plan and execute daily activities.
4. **Weight control**: strive to maintain a rational weight range
5. **Toxic substances**: avoid all toxic environments
6. **Preventive healthcare**: seek care regarding your genetics, family history, and environmental exposure.
7. **Curative healthcare**: seek and use appropriate therapy.
8. **Fasting:** enjoy its benefits for your body, mind, and soul.
9. **Appearance:** maintain good grooming, hygiene, and dress.
10. **Acceptance:** learn to improve and accept your body.

Your **MIND**

1. **Formal education:** complete your formal education program.
2. **Lifelong learning:** access programs for your continued education.
3. **Skills development:** develop and apply practical skills.
4. **Avoid negative input:** reduce your exposure to TV, the evening news, and tabloid newspapers.
5. **Read:** read quality, current periodicals and classic books.
6. **Write:** write letters, articles, and the book inside you.
7. **Music:** select and enjoy the inspirational power of music
8. **Motion pictures:** watch quality classic and current movies.
9. **Mentor and/or mentee:** share and/or gain knowledge.
10. **Volunteer:** share your skills and wisdom in friendly venues.

Your **SOUL**

1. **Know yourself:** consider that exciting Journey into the Self
2. **Humor:** take time to laugh, joke, and smile.
3. **Give God a chance:** nurture your spirituality.
4. **Time and recreation**: first take time for yourself *alone*.
5. **Positive attitude:** think and act positively.
6. **Know your passion:** find out what motivates you: follow your bliss.
7. **Deal with anger:** learn to deal with anger; let go; move on.
8. **Take reasonable risks:** optimize your life with good risk management.
9. **Balance your Life**: know when "enough is enough."
10. **Live in the moment:** yesterday is history; tomorrow, mystery; today, a gift.

7.1: GOALS: ULTRA-SHORT-TERM GOALS

List the ultra-short-term Goals you wish to achieve *immediately*.

Eliminate "toxic people"

Eliminate "toxic forces"

Eliminate "toxic environments"

Time-constrained opportunities or challenges

7.2: GOALS: SHORT-TERM (UP TO 1 YEAR)

List the Goals you wish to achieve in the next year.

1.

2.

3.

4.

5.

6.

7.

8.

9.

10.

7.3: GOALS: MID-TERM (UP TO 5 YEARS)

List the Goals you wish to achieve in the next 1-5 years.

1.

2.

3.

4.

5.

6.

7.

8.

9.

10.

7.4: GOALS: LONG-TERM (UP TO 10 YEARS)

List the Goals you wish to achieve in the next 10 years.

1.

2.

3.

4.

5.

6.

7.

8.

9.

10.

7.5: GOALS: *BEFORE YOU DIE*

List the Goals you wish to achieve before you die.

1.

2.

3.

4.

5.

6.

7.

8.

9.

10.

7.6: GOALS MATRIX: YOU

Organize your key Goals on this matrix.

YOUR...

Body

Mind

Soul

Competencies

7.7: GOALS MATRIX: YOUR WORLD

Organize your key Goals on this matrix.

YOUR WORLD...

Family

Friends

Employment/Education

Society

*"You
don't have
to be a fantastic
hero to do certain
things —to compete.
You can be just an ordinary
chap, sufficiently motivated
to reach challenging goals. The
intense effort, the giving of everything you've got, is a very pleasant bonus."*
—Sir Edmund Hillary

Chapter 8

What Is *The One-page Strategic Planner?*

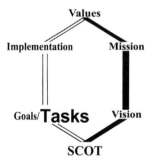

"Hi, I discovered the secret of life
at your bar, and I wrote it on a cocktail napkin ..."

Chapter 8
What Is *The One-page Strategic Planner?*
Optimizing your Life with its power of focus

"How do you eat an elephant?
One bite at a time."
—Elephant joke of the 1960s

Life is a complex journey of opportunities and challenges. Personal Goals make your journey smoother and more successful. Goals are key; they define your grand targets for your future. Goals specify the proper and efficient use of your time, energy, emotions, and resources. Well-defined, attainable "SMART" Goals increase your chances of successful completion.

One of the major reasons for frustration and failure of *organizational* strategic planning has been the creation and selection of Goals and then *Focused Action Plans* that are too grand, too large in scope to be completed. The premise on which *The One-page Strategic Planner* is based, is the division of any Goal into its component parts—or *projects;* and, in turn, the separation of each project into its component *tasks*. This process creates a *Goal-driven* hierarchy composed of a Goal and its projects and tasks. Each Goal will have a set of pertinent, rational, and attainable *Focused Tasks*.

GOAL
Projects
Focused Tasks

Each of the resultant tasks will certainly be smaller and more manageable. When properly defined and selected, each task can be successfully completed with the available resources in a short period of time. This "divide and conquer" concept of goals management is akin to the Japanese concept *kaizen*; i.e., where quality improvements are made in small steps. It also celebrates the human response wherein "success breeds success." This invariably leads to a positive view of strategic planning with its concomitant on-going support.

The Structure of *The One-page Strategic Planner*

The *One-page* itself is built around the "Top 10" Task Questions. Some of the questions are basic, obvious, and easy to answer; others are deeper and more complex, requiring more time, effort to answer, and space (See Worksheet 8.1).

The title box has areas for the entry of the Task along its related Project. There is space for entry of the name of the organization and the team, should others be involved in your *personal* strategic planning process.

Question #1 asks you to *define the specific Task*. This is perhaps the most important step.

Question #2 asks you to *define the current status of the Task*. Is it a totally new Task or an old Task being revisited? If the latter, give a brief history of the past efforts.

Question #3 asks you to *define success*. How will you know the Task has been completed successfully, even in part?

Question #4 asks you to *define who will be doing the work on the Task*. Most likely, you will be the champion of the efforts, perhaps working alone. If others are involved, list them and their roles.

Question #5 asks you to *define the actual steps involved in completing the Task*. If the numbers of steps increases to more than five, it may be wise to divide the Task into two or more Tasks.

Question #6 addresses the *resources necessary for successful completion of the Task*. You will need to determine which resources you have, which you lack, and how you plan to gain the missing resources. This question addresses the tangible assets needed, those that money (capital) can buy.

8.1: The *One-Page* Strategic Planner

Task_____
Org/Team, if any:_____ **Date:** _____
Goal:_____ **Project:**_____

---

1. What is the specific *Task?*

2. What is the *current status?*

3. What is the definition of *success?*

4. Who will *do it?* (champions and team)

5. What will the champion and the team *specifically do?*

6. What *resources* are needed/lacking?

7. What specific *challenges/hurdles* are expected?

8. When will the *Task* be done?

9. How will *progress, success, or failure* be evaluated and *measured?*

10. Who will *monitor the progress* and to whom will the *reports* be given?

Question #7 asks you to *define specific challenges or hurdles you anticipate at the outset.* This question tends to focus on people, within or outside your team. It asks which "benevolent" people may actually be "toxic" to you and the Task at hand.

Question #8 addresses the issue of time—*when the Task will be completed.* If a Task is simple and focused, a "best guess" estimate may suffice. However, in linking several Tasks within a given project, there may be a demand for the completion of one Task before another Task can even be started. You must maintain a hierarchy of Tasks in order to relate each task with its Project and, in turn, with its Goal.

Question #9 addresses the issue of measurement—that is, *how progress, success, or failure is evaluated and measured over time.* A well-defined Task should be readily subject to measurement—wherein success can also be defined.

Question #10 asks *who will monitor the progress and who will be given the reports.* This question addresses the location of "power" in an organization. For *personal* strategic planning, *you are the power*—and the completed Scorecard on each *One-page* will be your report.

Applying *The One-page Strategic Planner*

In the world of *personal* strategic planning, with its focus on one's body, mind, and soul, an example of a reasonable Goal might be:

Goal: To get my body in shape within nine months.
   This is certainly a laudable, yet large, Goal, which could easily be divided into its related projects, such as attaining:

Projects
   Project: Weight control (a rational weight range)
   Project: Muscle strength and tone
   Project: Bone, joint, and skin health

Beyond those obvious projects within the goal of "getting in shape," you could also add related projects such as:

Project: Hair style and grooming
Project: Daily personal hygiene
Project: Clothes

Tasks

The next step is to divide each project into focused, attainable Tasks. For example, weight control can be reduced to food choices, caloric intake, and physical exercise. Using the specific Task of "caloric intake" as an example, the *One-page* might look like the example on Worksheet 8.2.

The Scorecard

The *One-page* has been adapted to serve as a follow-up "scorecard" of progress, success, or failure during the Implementation process. The addition of columns to the right of the page are for specific dates/times. This Scorecard is an extension of the original *One-page*, allowing you to update any of the original or subsequent responses to the ten questions. By adding columns, even by pasting additional sheets of columns, to the right, one can maintain a broad view of the process all at one glance. (See Worksheets 8.3 and 8.4.)

The use of this format, this written scorecard, is key to the successful completion of any task. With the application of a table-based database such as is found in Microsoft Works or any number of available software packages, one can track the progress of implementation of any specific task with greater ease.

The *One-page* Goal/Project/Task hierarchy format can be adapted for all aspects of your *organizational* life as well as your *personal* strategic planning, including your own mind and soul, as well as all your relationships to your world, spouse, family, education, work, society, and even a Supreme Being.

A Hierarchy of Tasks

In order to manage a series of Tasks and their related Projects, as well as the ultimate Goal, you may wish to adapt Worksheet

8.2: The *One-Page* Strategic Planner

Task: Reduce caloric intake

You/Team/Org:___Self_____ Date:___15 Jan 2003_____

Goal:___Get body in shape___ Project:___Weight control_____

---

1. What is the specific *Task*?
To reduce and control my daily calorie intake

2. What is the *current status*?
I am _____ lbs. overweight which is _____% overweight based on my reasonable target weight range of _____ to _____ lbs.

3. What is the definition of *success*?
Reaching the target range of _____ to _____ lbs. in _____ months (date:_____)

4. Who will *do it*? (champion and team)
I am the Champion. I am in charge, I am responsible. I will seek advice/help/support from the following benevolent confidant(s) such as mate, nutritionist: _____.

5. What will the champion and the team *specifically do*?
I/we will learn about the calorie content of foods and portion control. I/we will create and follow a personalized food intake program. I will consider any safe and economical "gimmick" to assist me. I will celebrate all my efforts, and especially my successes.

6. What *resources* are needed/lacking?
In creating and following my program, I will obtain the necessary kitchen equipment. I will clean out, toss, or donate all foods outside the program.

7. What specific *challenges/hurdles* are expected?
I will gain ongoing private support from benevolent confidants, but avoid all "toxic" negative people and forces. I will stay on my new eating program until it becomes a beneficial long term habit.

8. When will the *Task* be done?
I expect that one-half the goal will be reached by _____(specific date) and the full goal by _____(date)

9. How will *progress, success, or failure* be evaluated and *measured*?
While I expect to see immediate results, I expect that the program will be a step-wise success over a period of time described above. The only arbitrator of success will be my weight scale.

10. Who will *monitor the progress* and to whom will the *reports* be given?
While my calorie control intake program is private, I will report to/seek support from my benevolent confidants _____.

8.5, "Hierarchy of Tasks" to your personal needs.

Author's Suggestions

If any Focused Task proves to be too big or complex to be completed on a timely basis, it can be split into two or more smaller tasks, using additional *One-pages.*

The copyrighted *Optimize Your Life!* worksheets may be enlarged and photocopied by the purchaser for limited *personal* use. The Interactive Worksheets CD includes all the worksheets.

To manage a large or increasing number of specific Tasks, organize them under each related hierarchical Project and Goal manually (adapting Worksheet 8.5) or via a database table for convenience.

The importance of maintaining the entire *Optimize Your Life!* process in writing cannot be overemphasized. The process of writing organizes and prioritizes your thoughts and decisions and will provide honest and complete information for the successful follow-up and completion of each task. Avoid the temptation to merely store this data in your mind. Over time, the mind will play tricks on you, and may undermine the attainment of your Tasks, Projects, and Goals.

"If you are not keeping score you are just practicing."
—Vince Lombardi, legendary coach

"Always remember that the future comes one day at a time."
—Dean Acheson, U.S. statesman

"A journey of a thousand miles
must begin with a single step."
—Lao-tzu

"Live as if you were to die tomorrow.
Learn as if you were to live forever."
—Mahatma Gandhi

"It is a mistake to look too far ahead. Only one link in the chain of destiny can be handled at a time."
—Winston Churchill

"Do not start vast projects with half-vast ideas."
—Bernhoff von Bergen

"Take-offs are optional. Landings are mandatory."
—Father Thomas A. Gude

"Strategic Planning is not rocket science, but without it there would be no rocket science."
—The Author

"By the mile it's a trial, by the yard it's hard, but by the inch it's a cinch."
—F. Fred Ferguson

Optimize Your Life!
Quick Results: <u>Tasks</u>

List three specific **tasks** you can finish in the very near future.

| 1. |
| 2. |
| 3. |

8.3: The *One-Page* Strategic Planner with Scorecard

Task_____

You/Team/Org:_____ **Date:** _____

Goal:_____ **Project:**_____

	Date	Date
1. What is the specific *Task?*		
2. What is the *current status?*		
3. What is the definition of *success?*		
4. Who will *do it?* (champions and team)		
5. What will the champion and the team *specifically do?*		
6. What *resources* are needed/lacking?		
7. What specific *challenges/hurdles* are expected?		
8. When will the *Task* be done?		
9. How will *progress, success, or failure* be evaluated and *measured?*		
10. Who will *monitor the progress* and to whom will the *reports* be given?		

8.4: The One-Page Follow-Up Scorecard
Task_____
Attach to the right of each *One-page.*

	Date	Date	Date	Date
1.				
2.				
3.				
4.				
5.				
6.				
7.				
8.				
9.				
10.				

8.5: Hierarchy of Tasks

GOAL: _____

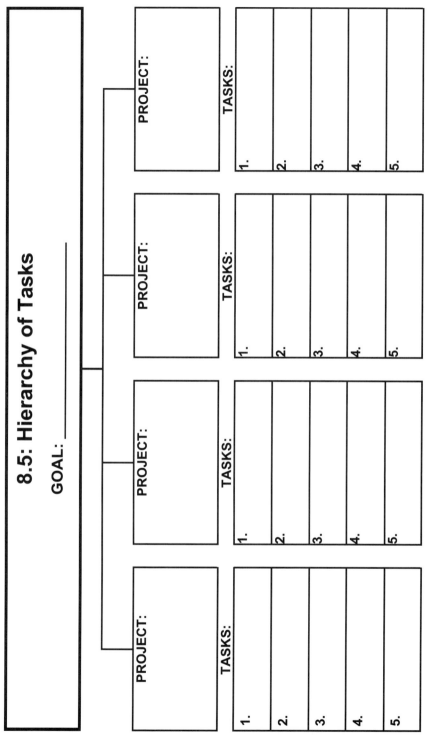

PROJECT:

TASKS:

1.
2.
3.
4.
5.

PROJECT:

TASKS:

1.
2.
3.
4.
5.

PROJECT:

TASKS:

1.
2.
3.
4.
5.

PROJECT:

TASKS:

1.
2.
3.
4.
5.

*"God grant me the serenity to accept
the things I cannot change,
the courage to change the things I can,
and the wisdom to know the difference."*
—Reinhold Niebuhr

Part III

The Tactics of Personal Planning

*"Start by doing what is necessary,
then what is possible, and suddenly
you are doing the impossible."*
—St. Francis of Assisi

"Try not. Do. Or do not. There is no try."
—Yoda, Jedi Master

Chapter 9

How Will You Complete Your Goals?

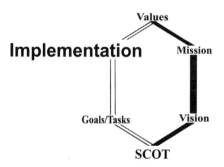

"What we think, or what we know, or what we believe, is, in the end, of little consequence. The only consequence is what we do."
—John Ruskin (1819-1900)

"Woulda, coulda, shoulda. Next!"

Chapter 9
How Will You Complete Your Goals?
Implementing your personal strategic plan

"We are fascinated by innovation,
but are resistant to change."
—Unknown

Part II addressed the cognitive or thinking aspects of personal strategic planning. That process analyzed "you and your world"; that is, it dissected you into manageable pieces. Then it put those pieces back together to synthesize the potential "new" you and your world in the form of a strategy, a strategic plan for your optimized future. Part III calls for action, both cognitive and physical, to complete your personal strategic plan by *Implementation* or tactics.

In the First Gulf War, General Colin Powell was the strategist, General Norman Schwarzkopf was the tactician.

In your world, you are both.

Implementation Process

Implementation is the final phase of the first round of personal or organizational strategic planning. The specific Focused Tasks are executed by you, possibly with the help of supportive people—your team. You will need to muster the skills, passion, and perseverance to complete each task. Some Tasks should be simple and can be completed in only days or weeks. The simpler the task, the better. Small incremental advances or changes are far more productive and valuable than grandiose and dramatic plans that often lead to frustration, delay, or failure.

Progress on some Tasks may falter and they may have to be reevaluated. This may require some Tasks to be altered or even abandoned. Other tasks may take a new track when additional information, resources, or hurdles are revealed during the process of Implementation. Recognizing this possibility of change, you may want to create contingency plans that can be put in place as soon as an insurmountable barrier is met. An alternate is to split a challenging task into two or more smaller tasks, and move on.

Being Your Own Change Agent

Earlier we noted that one definition of strategic planning, be it for an organization or an individual, is:

"The management of change."

For strategic planning to be of any benefit, it must lead to change. Your willingness to make changes in your life is a product of many factors, the most important being your past experiences. Your previous planning, efforts to change, and to take charge of your life are the key factors in any potential future change. If you succeeded, you might be ready for more changes. If you failed, your interest in change may be diminished.

Efforts for change may also be affected by your fears of the future, such as:

- fears of the known
- fears of the suspected
- fear of the unknown

As your own change agent, you may fear failure or even success and the demands that accompany success.

You may harbor fears of criticism that may arise, paradoxically, with either failure or success. There may be toxic forces or people in your life that want to keep you just as you are.

Beware the *self-fulfilling prophet,* who may reside within you and undermine your efforts. Replace its negative message with the positive mantra:

"Whatever you can do or dream you can, begin it.
Boldness has genius, power, and magic in it."
—Johann Wolfgang von Goethe

Even though you know the "what and why," some things should be done to improve your life. The energy to change must be mustered. Your source of personal power for change comes from many venues, both internal and external. The key factors are:

- motivation
- inspiration
- attitude
- positive thinking

There are times when the anticipated reward from the completion of a Goal or Project is enough to carry you through to the finish line. However, quite often, you need positive input from outside yourself, from a range of sources including religious and secular sermons, lectures, tapes, and books. Occasionally, the support of a mentor will suffice for success.

Managing Risk

A risk is defined as the possibility of suffering harm, loss, or danger. Risk-taking is a process of making a choice to take a chance at gaining something new at the risk of losing something you have.

Every day in your normal life, you take risks. Some are so automatic that they take the form of habits, both good and bad. You take risks as you travel, breathe air, consume food, drink water, and seek the apparent safety of your home.

You often make choices that include risk to advance your personal life or to improve your education, profession, or career. Sometimes, risk-taking may be a source of excitement or remedy for boredom.

Appropriate risk-taking—that is, risk management—is linked to many aspects of our past, present, and future lives. Your current willingness to take new risks is most prominently linked to your past successes or failures at risk-taking. At one extreme are the *risk averse folk,* whose motto is "Better safe than sorry." At the other extreme are the *risk tolerant people,* whose motto is, "Damn the torpedoes; full steam ahead." Most of your choices for appropriate risk management fall somewhere within these extremes.

Risk-taking is also closely linked to the successful use and application of *all* the phases of *Optimize Your Life!:* Values, Mission, and Vision Statements; SCOT Analysis; and definition and selection of Goals, Projects, and Tasks. Environmentalist John Muir noted:

"When we try to pick out anything by itself,
we find it hitched to everything else in the universe."

After you complete the process of the definition and selection of Goals, their component Projects, and Focused Tasks, evaluate each Task on its own *One-page* and answer the *One-page's* ten questions before you initiate action.

Inherent in the Focused Task-driven *One-page* is the fact that each Focused Task is an irreducible call for action (tactics or implementation), which in turn induces incremental units of change which are in turn related to small steps of risk-taking. Because each Focused Task is small, it can be rapidly completed so as to maintain momentum, success, and the real and psychological rewards of success. This process is risk management at its most efficient and safest.

Why Strategic Planning Fails

Success or failure at the Implementation phase is also linked to a wide range of factors. Included are the quality of the strategic plan and selection of specific tasks, as well as the skills and resources (time, energy, emotions, money, and the things money can buy) available to you. In addition, the incentives (rewards and recognition) for you in light of the risks involved are major factors. Last, but not least, is the effort applied in the Implementation (tactical) phase. Missing just one of these key factors may alter the outcome; missing two or more, will certainly lead to failure.

You have addressed on a personal basis not only Strategic Thinking and Planning (STP) but also personal skills and resources. As to incentives, the risk/reward ratio is a personal one in your strategic planning, one that can only be defined and applied by you. Without some degree of risk-taking, change is unlikely.

Outcomes in the Quest for *Change:* A Matrix of Success or Failure						
STP +	Skills +	Incentives +	Resources +	Action =		Change
NO	Yes	Yes	Yes	Yes =		Confusion
Yes	**NO**	Yes	Yes	Yes =		Anxiety
Yes	Yes	**NO**	Yes	Yes =		Apathy
Yes	Yes	Yes	**NO**	Yes =		Frustration
Yes	Yes	Yes	Yes	**NO** =		Business as usual

Adapted from Curtis Russell with permission.

Celebrate Your Efforts and Success

Since you are *the* leader, President, and Chief Executive Officer of your life, you provide the action for Implementation and monitor the progress of efforts on each specific task on a scheduled basis. You must have vision, skills, and passion for each of your specific tasks. You must maintain the written scorecard on each *One-page!* When any task is completed, celebrate your success. When effort is expended, even if success is not attained, celebrate anyway. Celebrate what you have learned and adapt it to your future efforts. Start by setting aside a specific time of the week for celebration, be it Friday after work or school, be it before or after your weekly religious or spiritual time.

Celebrate your efforts, your successes, and your life.

Author's Suggestions

Defining laudable Goals/Projects/Tasks for your personal strategic planning can be a relatively easy process, perhaps even fun. It takes time, effort, and introspection (sometimes a bit painfully) to read the text, to ponder the worksheets, to write down the answers to the questions, and then to define and select the Goals/Projects/Tasks. The hard part is beginning to act, to reach into the unknown to change your life and habits, and to take risks.

The *One-page* concept addresses these latter challenges by reducing your Implementation, your efforts as a tactician, to small Tasks—to small steps for change, and to small increments of risk.

The awesome power of classic Goal-setting can be applied successfully by reducing each Goal down to manageable and attainable tasks, to small bites, to small steps. Lao-tzu noted:

> *"A journey of a thousand miles*
> *must begin with a single step."*

In Old French, we find the original meaning of the word "journey" to be "the distance one can walk in just one day." In the past when strategic planning failed, it was often because its adherents tried to do too much too fast... and became disillusioned and abandoned the process.

> *"Carpe diem." ("Seize the day.")*
> —Horace

> *"Our greatest glory is not in never failing,*
> *but in rising every time we fall."*
> —Kung-fu Tzu (Confucius)

> *"Take time to deliberate, but when the time for action has arrived, stop thinking and go in."*
> —Napoleon Bonaparte

> *"Results! Why, man, I have gotten a lot of results.*
> *I know several thousand things that won't work."*
> —Thomas A. Edison

> *"There is a difference between knowing the path*
> *and walking the path."*
> —Morpheus, *The Matrix*

<u>On Perseverance</u>

*"Press on: nothing in the world can
take the place of perseverance.*

*Talent will not; nothing is more common
than unsuccessful men with talent.*

*Genius will not; unrewarded
genius is almost a proverb.*

*Education will not; the world
is full of educated derelicts.*

*Persistence and determination
alone are omnipotent."*

—Calvin Coolidge

*"Success is simply a matter of luck.
Ask any failure."*
—Earl Wilson

Chapter 10

What Can Help
You Succeed?

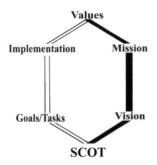

"Take charge of your destiny..."
—Jack Welch, former CEO
of General Electric

Chapter 10
What Can Help You to Succeed?
Encouraging you to act

"Anything inside that immobilizes me, gets in my way,
keeps me from my goals, is all mine."
—Wayne Dyer, psychologist

You and Your Universe

The universe is driven by repetitive cycles, rhythms, and orbital patterns as well as random cosmic phenomena. On Earth, daily and seasonal cycles are linked with complex and integrated biological "clocks" and "programs" throughout the plant and animal kingdoms. Together these phenomena make the future largely unpredictable and uncontrollable. However, only humans may be able to act to modify, transcend, or augment these cycles and phenomena, by implementing their *free will,* long-term strategic planning to address the future and its inherent change.

You are a product of that universe, a product of your parents and your ancestors, as well as your early environment. Above all, you are human. You have capabilities far above the lower animals. You can think logically. You can use words and concepts. You can envision the future. You play a key role in influencing, even controlling, your destiny.

However, as a human you come into the world with a genetic code given to you by others. You came into a world that you did not choose and lived an early life in a world you could not control except by crying. You were at the mercy of your world that gave you both opportunities or challenges, a good or bad life—but above all, your values.

Only as you approached adulthood could you take some charge of your life and your destiny. During this transition, you became responsible for your actions and behavior, your successes or failures, and the expression of your values.

Human Values and Survival

What are sources of our human values? One can start by looking at the values of ancient humans, whose values were linked to one primary goal, survival. Humans were created by God (based on the concept of teleology) or evolved (à la Darwin and others), or by a combination of the two—take your choice. Most scholars feel that forerunners to humans evolved over millions of years.

Eventually *Homo erectus* was the first human that *stood* on Earth. Later, perhaps much later, *Homo sapiens sapiens* arrived and were the first to truly *think.* During this long interval, individuals, family units, and small clans roamed the Earth as nomads, hunting and gathering. In order for these ancient humans, our ancestors, to survive, they needed to fight, kill, steal, and hoard. Those who survived expressed behaviors that became linked with their values.

We are their descendants... their survivors.

On Civility

Much later, about 10,000 years ago, the Agricultural Revolution started in southeastern Turkey in the Karakadag Mountains, where einkorn, a variant of wheat was first propagated. Soon nomadic tribes and clans were able to settle down and develop societies. During these past ten millennia, especially during the past five, new philosophies, monotheistic Western religions, and societies have tried to instill a degree of civility in humans.

The efforts to attain civility were first introduced in the Code of Hammurabi, and later in the Old Testament of the Bible as the Ten Commandments. It is interesting to note that four Commandments dealt with our love of God, while six guided and assisted us in our relationships with our fellow man. The Ten Commandments and the Golden Rule all focus upon behaviors, rather than principles, that express one's inner values.

The Role of Values

As noted in Chapter 4, the way to decode a person's values is to study his behavior:

$$B = f(V + E)$$

Behavior is a *function* of your **Values** and your **Environment**.

While your values drive every thought you have, every word you utter, every decision you make, and everything you do, your current environment also plays a key role. Your true values may be expressed through less than civil behavior in times of catastrophes such as war, famine, or natural disasters. In times when irresponsibility is rampant, what do you do in light of—or in spite of—your values? The formula may also ask the question:

"What is your behavior, in light of your values,
when you think that no one is looking?"

Since your values were largely given to you by your parents and environment during your early years, what can you do to change them?

In Chapter 3, you addressed the cognitive processes of *self-analysis of real life experiences* and *values clarification.* It appears that while we may not be able to change our values, we can successfully work to modify our behavior and responses to these values.

During my life and studies, I have seen major permanent behavioral changes in individuals as a result of one or more of three key factors:

1. An environmental catastrophe (like war or famine)
2. A serious illness (acute or chronic)
3. A deep religious experience

Over the millennia hundreds of values have been defined including the *core, internal,* and *external* values discussed in Chapter 3. Society has developed laws and regulations based on these values in order to create and maintain social order. The role and power of any value in a given society changes from time to time, from location to location. Even today, in the 21st Century, values and their resultant customs, regulations, and laws are far from uniform throughout the world.

Beyond Cynicism

In the process of studying our ancient values that focused on survivability and our very recent quest for civility, we can easily become cynical. The history of all human endeavor is filled with a boundless capacity for cynicism no matter the topic—politics, business, education, even religion (perhaps especially religion). The more we study and the more we watch the History Channel, the more we learn to support this position.

September 11, 2001 may have crystallized our cynicism.

Each of us is a product of millions of years of selection by survival. Our ancestors were the successful ones; they survived. The weak, the unlucky, died. At times of life-threatening crises we are all focused at the ultimate level, self-preservation. That does not make us evil—just successful.

Ten thousand years of some sort of civility among humans is a microscopic segment of time in the history of humans. In spite of that overwhelming ratio of civility-to-survivability, humans have done fairly well. Over six billion people live on the Earth, and there is not full-scale war all the time. There is an amazing degree of law and order. Given the ancient nature of humans, that is success.

However, we can do better.

The Hope of Love and Forgiveness

Where do we go from there? We struggle with this cynicism amidst wanting to survive and be civil at the same time. For me, that Quest is found in that list of *external values,* it comes from my Judeo-Christian upbringing. The message is simple, functional, and memorable: the word is love. It is the foundation of the message of Jesus of Nazareth:

> *"A new commandment I give unto you,*
> *That ye love one another; as I have loved you."*

In the New Testament, we are admonished to love one another, to love even the unlovely.

Love goes well beyond Christianity. In his book *Oneness: Great Principles Shared by All Religions* the Dalai Lama observes:

> *"Every major religion of the world has
> similar ideas of love."*

However, love has a correlate: forgiveness. The power of love is magnified by the power of forgiving others as we are forgiven. We are all frail, we are all humans, and we all need to forgive, as we need to be forgiven:

> *Take heed to yourselves: If thy brother trespass against
> thee, rebuke him; and if he repent, forgive him.*
> —Luke 17:3

Forgiveness is also a powerful part of many philosophies and all major religions. It is difficult and often risky to ask someone for forgiveness or to forgive someone. There is a cynical but poignant bumper sticker that reads:

> *"Jesus loves you, everyone else thinks you're an a------."*

Bishop Desmond Tutu of South Africa wrote of the story of apartheid which documents decades of atrocities. His book is entitled *No Future without Forgiveness.*

The Awesome Power of Self-Forgiveness

In this book we have traveled a long way together. Let us take a moment to look at an even deeper level in this world of forgiveness. We need to address the challenge of gaining forgiveness from the potentially most unforgiving person in our lives. We need to gain forgiveness from ourselves. We need to allow ourselves to "let go" of things we did that we wish we had not done and to forgive ourselves for the things we wish we had done but failed to do. We are often our own worst critics, and whether we realize it or not, this criticism can paralyze us.

There is a wonderful book entitled *Forgiving Yourself* by Beverly Flanigan, M.S.S.W. This must-read has a subtitle that speaks for itself: "A step-by-step guide to making peace with your mistakes and getting on with your life."

Self-Acceptance

Optimize Your Life! is focused on the key premise: know yourself. It takes great effort and insight to honestly complete that inventory of self-knowledge. In the process of personal strategic planning, it would be wonderful if you could also learn to accept yourself for who you are—your strengths and challenges, your magnificence and frailties.

While this process of self-acceptance may be facilitated by personal strategic planning, it may take outside effort on the part of qualified professionals and/or supportive friends. This process is, by definition, self-focused, but is not selfish. The rewards for gaining self-knowledge and self-acceptance are many. You can free yourself of negative and debilitating forces. You can learn to love yourself, which is a requisite to learning to love others.

"No one can make you feel inferior
without your consent."
—Eleanor Roosevelt

Moving Towards the Future

Regardless of who you are, what you have, or what you do, you possess the greatest gift of all: life. Whether you are young or old, rich or poor, physically strong or weak, well-educated or not, you have the same potential for an optimized life. Using the power of *Optimize Your Life!,* you can evaluate your current situation via your Values and Mission Statements and your SCOT analysis. You can address your future through your Vision Statement. You can pull all this together to define and select reasonable and rational goals, both short-term and long-term.

By choosing key short-term Goals and dividing them into Projects and Tasks, you can start Implementing these Tasks immediately. You will be successful. You will start taking control of your life, your destiny. You need to update the worksheets of *Optimize Your Life!* This repetitive process will yield new and better information about yourself and your world, so that you can choose better Goals/Projects/Tasks and Implement them. Above all, you need to celebrate your efforts as well as your successes.

While you will never gain a truly "clean slate" for your life, you can identify the good and the bad aspects of your life; then jettison the bad and support the good. Most of us cannot run away with the circus; we have responsibilities to our families, to society, perhaps to a Supreme Being. Above all, we have the ultimate responsibility to ourselves.

One tangential benefit of the process of *personal* strategic planning is gathering data about yourself and your world, about your possessions, your activities, your frustrations, and your successes. This database will make it easier for you to collect, evaluate, sort, and even toss out a large number of entities, from assets to liabilities, from acquaintances to enemies, from benevolent to toxic forces, etc.

You can discover what is really *important* to you. You can truly clean up your life, your clutter. You can carry out a personal garage sale! In the process you may choose to simplify your life. You can gain a balance between having too much stuff and simply being. You can balance your life. You can ask and answer the question: "When is enough, enough?" You may decide to follow the increasingly popular maxim:

"Live simply so that others may simply live."

You can also find out what gives you satisfaction and happiness. About one hundred years ago, Italian industrial engineer and economist Valfredo Pareto was interested in the interrelationships of economy and society. He studied the distribution of wealth, the "haves and have nots," noting that 80% of the wealth was controlled by 20% of the population. This pattern was found to be true worldwide, and constant over many decades. Pareto's 80/20 "law" has been applied to many facets of the world of business and professional life. It is stated that 80% of profits come from 20% of customers; 80% of complaints come from 20% of clients; 80% of time is spent on 20% of goods and services; and 80% of absenteeism is assignable to 20% of employees.

Pareto's Law can be applied to your personal life as well: if 80% of your joys come from 20% of your acquaintances, then 80% of the grief comes from 20% of the people in your life. The great challenge, of course, is when 80% of both your joy and grief come from the same 20% of your world—some call this marriage, others parenthood, and others employment.

What Is a Successful Life?

Simply stated, a successful life may be:

- living in a place that is safe and enjoyable
- with people who provide mutual respect and love
- doing things that are rewarding and satisfying
- having enough things to meet your needs
- and in a society that recognizes everyone's individuality, freedom, and independence.

Wow... how are you doing? Is your life now close to that utopian ideal, or is it at least approaching it?

There are also many wise, even clever, mottoes for life in the world literature, such as:

"To laugh often and much; to win the respect of intelligent people and the affection of children; to earn the appreciation of honest critics and endure the betrayal of false friends; to appreciate beauty, to find the best in others; to leave the world a little better, whether by a healthy child, a garden patch or a redeemed social condition; to know even one life has breathed easier because you have lived. This is the meaning of success."
—Ralph Waldo Emerson

"Fear less, hope more;
Whine less; breathe more;
Talk less, say more;
Hate less, love more;
And all good things are yours."
—Swedish proverb

There are also short, easy-to-remember mottoes, such as:

"Learn from yesterday,
live for today,
hope for tomorrow."
—Bernhoff von Bergen

"Think.
Believe.
Dream.
Dare."
—Walt Disney

Perhaps you would like to create your own life motto, based on your current life and values, and your dreams, hopes, and plans for the future.

Why not share it with others? See page 196 for an avenue to focus your life and express yourself.

In Closing and Moving On

The metaphorical cards of life that you were dealt—i.e., your genetics and early life environment—were out of your hands, out of your control. How you "play" these cards is greatly influenced by your values and circumstances, most of which have also been given to you and were also out of your control to a great extent.

Most of our values are driven by our historical need to survive, yet society wants you to have and to express those values that support civility. What a challenge! What baggage we carry! For in the end, we are all held accountable. Society holds us responsible for everything we do!

In closing, I would like to share a poem from Apollinaire that addresses the opportunity, challenges, and risks of modern life. I offer it to the most advantaged people in the history of the human race—you and me. We have been given the greatest gift of all: life.

What have we done with these gifts? What will we do with them today, tomorrow, and all the tomorrows we are given?

From Apollinaire:

> *"Come to the edge of the cliff," he said.*
> *"No, we are afraid!"*
> *"Come to the edge of the cliff," he said.*
> *"No, we are afraid!"*
> *"Come to the edge of the cliff," he said.*
> *They came…*
> *he pushed them…*
> *they flew!*

Epilogue

"Those who know do not speak.
Those who speak do not know."
—Lao Tzu
(I hope this does not apply to *those who write.*)

Cathy © 1998 Cathy Guisewite. Reprinted by permission of Universal Press Syndicate. All rights reserved.

Epilogue

"May you live every day of your life."
—Jonathan Swift

Life is an adventure. The trip may be one of joy, satisfaction, challenges, and struggles, as well as successes and failures. The ultimate destination is death. While the young may deny it, most of us anticipate death with fear. A limited few seek death. They may be plagued with terminal disease or intolerable circumstances under destructive, environmental, political, or military forces. While death is inevitable, it is rarely a reasonable goal unto itself.

Some philosophies and religions view this life on Earth as only a transient period, and not an end unto itself, with the major emphasis on an afterlife (for example, Heaven). Others view this process as a repetitive one, with an eventual arrival at a final destination (such as Nirvana). While these approaches may be true, they certainly cannot be proven. Since it is possible that life is an end unto itself, the question should be posed:

*Why not optimize **this** life?*

On the Search for Happiness

From Aristotle to Freud and beyond there has been an abiding interest in the appropriate role of seeking pleasure and avoiding pain, and in the search for happiness in human life. Over the millennia, in philosophy, religion, and later in psychology, there has been a considerable range of debate regarding the importance of happiness in life, let alone the search for pleasure.

Hedonism (from the Greek *hedone,* pleasure) was popularized by a group of philosophical schools started by Aristippus of Cyrene (435-366 B.C.) which taught that pleasure is the ultimate goal in life. Subsequently Epicurus of Samos (342-268 B.C.) developed his school of philosophy, which included his own views on ethics, physics, biology, and logic. There was, however, a focus on the importance of minimizing pain and maximizing pleasure in the search for a happy life on earth.

Over the millennia the original message of Epicurus has been reduced and misused to:

"Eat, drink, and be merry, for tomorrow you may die!"

This is unfortunate, for Epicurus taught that the search for happiness included both the sensual (the five senses of seeing, tasting, touching, smelling, and hearing) and the higher forms of enjoyment such as mental activities, family, friendship, and ethical living. More important is his message that we should not pursue a pleasure that produces an excessive resultant pain—he uses sex as an example. However, he also noted that some pain and self-restraint is important for a happy life.

During the ensuing millennia, interest in Hedonism waxed and waned, but reached its zenith in Imperial Rome when Rome was looting the world and the decades of plenty were enjoyed at many levels of Roman society. Hedonism tends to flourish during times of plenty, at least when there is plenty for some segment of the population.

Erasmus (1466-1536 A.D.), and later Thomas More (1478-1535 A.D.), revived Hedonism, and David Hume (1711-1776 A.D.) adapted it to a form labeled "utilitarianism."

Coincident with the development of hedonism was another series of schools of philosophy, the Stoics, the first one started by Zeno of Citium (344-262 B.C.). The Stoics, who got their name from their meeting place, the *stoa poikele,* a decorated porch, in the Agora in Athens. The Stoics did not create new ideas but adapted the established concepts of philosophy, of the logic, physics, and ethics to develop practical dogmas for life. They looked to the reality of the laws of human nature and the cosmos in order to regulate their lives.

Stoic logic included the concept of *apatheia* (not to be confused with the meaning of the modern word *apathy*) which was an active process to deny oneself undisciplined emotions or passions, and foster reason, rational thinking. Therefore the goal in life is to live in harmony with human nature, and the cosmos.

Over the ensuing millennia, the message of the Stoics has, unlike the Epicureans, been fairly well maintained, namely that "to control one's emotions and passions, and live a rational life." They also taught that happiness was not attainable during this life on earth. Famous Stoics include Roman philosopher Epictetus (55-135 A.D.) as well as Roman emperor and philosopher Marcus Aurelius Antoninus (121-180 A.D.). Later, Stoicism and its focus on the laws of the cosmos led to *pantheism* (God in everything), which is strikingly in conflict with the Christian concept of one god in only three parts.

Stoicism and its view of cosmic and natural law fit well with Roman Law during its cycles of expansion, but especially during times of decline. Although the Stoics had an "idea of god," it was the introduction of the Hebrew concept of one providential God that Stoicism served as a bridge to Christianity. The Stoics and the early Christians viewed evil as a departure from the natural or essential nature of mankind.

You may choose to focus on a primarily "Epicurean" style of life, optimizing (not maximizing) the sensual pleasures of your life, without overdoing.

Or, you may select the "Stoic" style, wherein your life is based on reasoning (logic) and your efforts in controlling your emotions and passions.

In reality, your choice will be based on the "hard-wired" aspects of your personal history, values, and personality, along with your environment. You will most likely end up with a combination of the two basic styles of life, which can change from time to time, especially as you age.

Making Choices

After the story of Creation, the next story in the Bible is that of Adam and Eve in the Garden of Eden. God gave them free will—choice—and they used it by choosing to eat the fruit of the Tree of the Knowledge of Good and Evil. Although they were cast out of Eden into a tumultuous and dangerous world, God continued to grant them the power of choice in their lives.

Unfortunately, many human adults, however, fail to use that power to make wise choices, choosing instead to live spontaneous and ill-directed lives—making decisions by default.

Some have turned themselves over to the strict and orderly lives in religious or military institutions, wherein choice is limited. Others follow gurus and cult leaders, while some latch on to the latest craze or fad in education, business, or organizational life. For all these people, the decisions in life are made by others, and their personal need to think, plan, and choose is largely irrelevant. Many find comfort in that world, for a season, a decade or two, or even for life.

Some people focus their decisions on planning and executing vacations, the highlight of their year. There is, however, an important group of people who do take charge of their lives and plan, in part or full, for their education, career, marriage, family, and relationships with society and God.

These studies have shown that less than 5% of educated Americans use a written *personal* strategic planning program in their lives on a regular, ongoing basis. They also show that planners are generally more successful with finances, social relationships, family life, and personal growth, development, and satisfaction.

Focusing on You

Only if you take control of your life can you truly love yourself and enjoy high self-esteem. Then, and only then, can you successfully relate to others around you—be it at home or away.

Aristotle defined a virtuous life and one's ethics, based on his observations of what the noble and wise men of his time chose to do. He noted that the chief end—the highest good of all—is life. He described *means* as things done to produce something else, but *ends* as intrinsically valuable—the ultimate Goals. Although many ends are only means to further ends, one's aspirations and desires must have some final objective or pursuit. That chief end is a life of *happiness*, which, of course, varies from person to person based on their own human nature and personal experience. Of the twelve virtues Aristotle defined, he chose as the "crown virtue" magnanimity (pride); that is, one's appropriate level of self-esteem, self-love, and self-interest.

While I was in medical school and residency, and some were playing in the fields of Woodstock, Ayn Rand was lecturing and writing on her political and social views. Born and educated in the Soviet Union under Stalin, she came to the United States in the 1930s. She wrote plays, novels, and later political essays. Her focus was based on a "right-wing" conservative philosophy that she called *objectivism*—a term also used by Aristotle.

Objectivism, which is based on rational thinking and logic, has had periods of popularity in the history of philosophy and politics since Aristotle, namely Medieval Aristotelians and Baruch Spinoza. Rand reawakens objectivism in her books, including *The Virtue of Selfishness: A New Concept of Egoism.* It is based on a series of scripts and essays, noting that selfishness, in a positive sense, should be a prime motivator in successful living.

Rand expresses herself clearly when she defines selfishness as a concern for one's own interests—as compared to altruism, where one's life is given over entirely to others. Like Aristotle, her focus is on human life, the ultimate goal. For Rand, the key values are *reason, purpose,* and *self-esteem.* Her corresponding virtues (the acts by which one gains and/or keeps a value) are *ra-*

tionality, productiveness, and *pride.*

Rand goes on to define the ultimate human as a rational person who uses no physical force against others, except in retaliation, and only to the initiator of the physical force. Her view of the proper moral purpose of government is to provide only police, armed forces, and laws to protect people—and especially the people's rights to personal property.

Where Rand is most controversial is her attitude about helping others. She states that one should only help a stranger in an emergency situation.

Robert J. Ringer, from the world of business, wrote a number one bestseller, *Looking Out For #1.* In his book, he echoes the concepts of Aristotle and Rand in a pleasant, story-like motif, using a turtle mascot who addresses a series of "hurdles" in life's struggles. Of interest is his view of relating or dealing with self and others, noting that both a personal life and a social life are necessary. However, he recommends dealings with others be based on two essential ingredients: admiration or respect, and providing value for value in each relationship. He goes on to say that in all of life, including relationships, "everything worthwhile has a price."

Unfortunately, the modern use of the term *selfish* has such a powerfully negative connotation that it should be replaced by a term such as *self-focused,* which expresses a positive view. Whether or not you agree with the concept of selfishness by Rand and Ringer, reading them can be rewarding.

Others in Your Life

Humans are, by nature, social. They crave friendship. While individuals have made spectacular discoveries for society, the wide application of these advances were carried out by groups—even masses.

Individual humans need other humans for purposes of safety, productivity, procreation, and as Aristotle noted, to gain the number one reason for living: happiness. Aristotle also noted that there were three types of friendship:

1. Friendship based on mutual pleasure. When the pleasure is gone, the friendship is over.
2. Friendship based on mutual benefit or advantage. This is the classic business relationship, which ends when that benefit ends.
3. Friendship based on mutual goodness between equals. This is the most difficult friendship to create and maintain. It is the only friendship based on true love.

While the challenges and opportunities to "know ourselves" is great, it is even more difficult to "know others" and to meld them into our lives. However, the effort and risk, coupled with clear Aristotelian logic, is usually worth it.

Over the past two and a half millennia, there have been countless stories, poems, and how-to books written about human relationships and how to create and maintain great ones. You are encouraged to visit that wonderful world of literature and choose those that inspire you.

According to Aristotle, friendliness is a virtue and the mechanism that will allow one to develop friendship. He also notes that while friendship is key for a happy life, one also needs to have good health, opportunities to practice a moral and intellectual life, adequate resources, and good luck.

We are admonished to "love your neighbor as yourself" (Matthew 19:19). This concept is well demonstrated in the story of the Good Samaritan (Luke 10:25-37). The great love chapter of the Bible, I Corinthians 13, is popularized in weddings worldwide.

Jesus of Nazareth gave us a very clear message as regards the love of others:

"Greater love hath no man than this, that
he lay down his life for his friends."

Merging East and West

In any project or process, it is always good to look at apparent opposites, for life is full of pairs. There is up and down, yin and yang, dark and light, left and right, and even good and evil. There can be no good without evil. The concept of strategic planning is based on logic, which came largely from ancient Greece. When we look as the Eastern world, we find similar logic in the efforts of Confucius—a bureaucrat, not a religious leader—who created a system of linguistic, ethical, and legal conventions to establish and maintain social order. There is little spontaneity in either of these Eastern and Western traditions.

While strategic planning is a logical process, there should be times when an individual simply abandons strategic planning and the maximizing of life and possessions. It is rather time to "let go, smell the roses, and simply daydream." The Zen Buddhists would encourage us, at times, to simply:

Sit quietly... doing nothing.

On Being Alone

In October 1999, just after presenting a workshop on "The *One-page* Strategic Planner" in Portland, Maine, I drove to Mt. Washington, New Hampshire, for a weekend of hiking. Since it was raining, my usual hiking buddies opted out. I tried to link up with a hiking club, to no avail.

I headed out in the rain, alone, up Tuckerman's Ravine and then towards the Alpine Garden Trail on my way to the Auto Road and home. The light rain turned into giant snowflakes. A veritable winter wonderland had replaced a dreary fall day. I was lured into a bright winter hike, and continued on for over an hour in spite of a marked increase in the wind.

Then, "whiteout" conditions forced me to stop next to a huge cairn (a pile of rocks marking the trail) to wait out the storm. I climbed into my aluminized material bivvy sack and realized that I had my cell phone with me. I made a series of increasingly frustrating 911 calls, which left me wondering if my rescuers would come, let alone find my location.

As snow accumulated on my bivvy sack, I became concerned that my rescuers would not see me, so I slowly inched my up onto the surface of the snow and opened the end of my bivvy sack to evaluate my changing world. Unfortunately, gusts of wind filled my sack and, in spite of my efforts, tore it from my body. Now it me in a fall hiking outfit in an area known as "the home of the worst weather in the world" (April 12, 1934 wind speed: 231 miles per hour).

During that long night, with wind speeds up to 98 miles per hour, I waited for rescue, and eventually, having given up hope, I waited for death. As a physician, I had developed a professional relationship with "death and dying," but not a personal relationship with *my* dying—not with my death.

Around midnight, my rescuers came, took me off the mountain to a regional hospital for treatment of frost injuries, hypothermia, and rhabdomyolysis (the breakdown of muscle tissue due to voluntary and involuntary muscle flexing in an attempt to prevent/treat hypothermia).

Soon after my discharge from the hospital, Husson College in Maine invited me to share my experience and what I had learned the hard way. My presentation was entitled:

"Lessons for Living from a Mt. Washington Misadventure"

...which offered three admonitions, pieces of advice:
1. Be prepared to die!
2. Have a plan to live! (Yes—strategic planning!)
3. Do it now!

This presentation was recorded and broadcast on National Public Radio in New England, and I was invited to share my story in a range of speaking venues. About a year later, The Learning Channel coaxed me into a reenactment on Mt. Washington, and as a result of worldwide broadcasts, my new speaking career has skyrocketed. With support from Mark Victor Hansen of the *Chicken Soup for the Soul* book series fame, I am writing the accompanying "misadventure book."

I had enjoyed a lifetime of mountaineering with ascents on Kilimanjaro in Africa, Popo and Ixta in Mexico, Aconcagua in Argentina, and Elbrus in Russia. I had been in worse circumstances regarding high altitude, on steep glaciers with deadly crevasses, in deep snow, and in high winds. But on Mt. Washington, I was all alone. On the mountain, I had abundant time to think about dying—and to think about living. It was Boswell who wrote:

"The threat of hanging [dying] tends to focus the mind."

That time alone on that surrealistic Mt. Washington quest, that near-death experience, made me realize that in the long run, we will all be alone. We may now have a fine family, friends, and associates, but eventually, each of us will travel alone into that "ether," or whatever is out there.

It has been said since ancient times that:

"To know how to live, one must first learn how to die."

During that long night, in spite of hypothermia, my mind was clear. It was an opportunity to look deep into my religious beliefs and how I viewed death and what, if anything, would follow. My life had been greatly influenced by the teachings of Jesus of Nazareth. When one simply follows a religious or philosophical leader, as a guru or a savior, it is that leader who has done the initial work, perhaps even to the extreme of giving his life for the follower. It is the responsibility of the follower, the adherent, to take charge of his life, including his spiritual life.

In simple terms for the Christian, one can take Christ as his Savior, a contribution made completely by Him. The next step, to adhere to His teachings and to make Him the "Lord of your life," is your responsibility.

Strategic planning can be a powerful tool in this regard.

Taking Your Journey into the Self

In his book *The Hero with a Thousand Faces,* Joseph Campbell noted that there is a commonality among myths from throughout time and place. Campbell noted that there are generally three phases of the quest in mythology: *departure, initiation,* and *return.* These phases, or *rites of passage,* may be started by a "call to adventure" and evolve through a series of thresholds: the possibility of meeting interesting characters, of gaining supernatural aids or assistance, then rescue, and finally return. The quest takes the hero into a new and unknown world of trials and testing, and back home.

The hero always travels solo. However, a true hero who returns from a quest dies as an ordinary person and is reborn as a new or eternal person. The returning hero has changed and then lives a new life, for he then lives in two worlds.

Perhaps now is the time to make an effort to understand yourself, to give yourself permission to love yourself, to forgive yourself, to take that exciting, mysterious, and sometimes dangerous Journey into the Self. Out of that quest will emerge a better person—better able to address the challenges and opportunities of life, the joys and the sorrows of life, the risks and rewards of life, and the lives of those around you.

While none of us can join Gawain in the search for the Holy Grail, we can, however, optimize our ongoing strategic planning process by way of adventures or expeditions at home or in foreign lands. These ventures may allow us a controlled amount of stress, which in turn may encourage us to look within ourselves and our values. You do not have to go to an extreme of such a misadventure as I experienced in order to gain insights about yourself.

The Journey into the Self is an extended lifelong quest. Properly executed, each of us can create a unique life story. It has been said, that in the entire world, over all the ages, there are only two story themes:

1. Local citizen leaves town.
2. Stranger comes to town.

Your life can be a story of both.

"Follow your bliss."
—Joseph Campbell

"...I can only show you the door.
You're the one that has to walk through it."
—Morpheus, *The Matrix*

"Life is God's gift to you.
What you do with it is your gift to God."
—Reverend John Hagee

"...a world where anything is possible.
Where we go from here is
a choice I leave to you."
—Neo, *The Matrix*

The Ultimate *One-page* Strategic Planner

On the facing page is an attempt to *really* focus on one's life, to select and prioritize things you want to do which may be general Goals, more specific Projects, or *very* specific Tasks.

You may choose to create this worksheet after reading the book, completing the worksheets, and considerable deliberation.

An alternative is to start here and go wild, simply entering the first things that come to your mind. Remember that you can always return to the sheet and update and upgrade it.

Most of all, enjoy the Ultimate One-page Strategic Planner.

The Ultimate *One-Page* Strategic Planner

The Top 10 "To-Do" List for ME

1.	6.
2.	7.
3.	8.
4.	9.
5.	10.

The Top 10 "To-Do" List for close/intimate friends or spouse

1.	6.
2.	7.
3.	8.
4.	9.
5.	10.

The Top 10 "To-Do" List for family and friends

1.	6.
2.	7.
3.	8.
4.	9.
5.	10.

The Top 10 "To-Do" List for society

1.	6.
2.	7.
3.	8.
4.	9.
5.	10.

Possible Keys to an Optimum Life

Know yourself
Maintain your body
Expand your mind
Enlighten your soul
Give God a chance
Enjoy solitude
Meditate and pray
Communicate
Accept limitations
Adjust expectations
Eliminate "toxic" forces
Know your world
Live an examined life
Take reasonable risks
Make wise choices
Live life fully
Forgive yourself...
and others
Focus on being
Plan for tomorrow...
but live for today
Celebrate your efforts
Rejoice in your successes
Smile and laugh

*"If I had no sense of humor, I would have
long ago committed suicide."*
—Mahatma Gandhi

Appendix

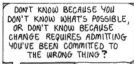

O.K., Time for Cynics, Skeptics, Smart-Alecks, Whiners...

In ancient Greece, for several hundred years prior to Socrates, there were philosophers, the *cynics,* who believed self-control was the only avenue to virtue. Over the centuries, the term "cynic" has evolved to a meaning of "faultfinder," since many of the original cynics excessively criticized their fellow man. Some sects of the cynics felt there was no truth that could be proven; they were the original skeptics.

Cathy Thorne © www.everyday people cartoons. com

AN UNEXAMINED LIFE MAY NOT BE WORTH
LIVING, BUT EXAMINING MINE IS EXHAUSTING.

First, I **do not** want to do strategic planning because:
___Too much work ___Too personal ___Violates my privacy
___Too vague ___Too specific ___Too detailed
___Asks too many questions ___Makes me look at myself
___Dredges up "stuff" ___Forces me to make rational decisions
___Makes me examine my world ___Points out "toxic" forces
___It didn't work at the office ___factory ___church _____
___Other _____ ___Other _____

"Wisdom" for the Cynics and Skeptics

Self
Avoid comparison. A false sense of self-esteem is better than none at all.
Which is worse, ignorance or apathy? *–I don't know and I don't care.*
I may be schizophrenic, but at least I have each other.
Nothing improves with age.
Those who cannot laugh at themselves leave the job to others.
Scientists say one out of four people is crazy. Check three friends. If they're
    O.K., you're not.
As I resolve my guilt, I am in touch with my inner sociopath.
I revel in my personality flaws; without them I'd have no personality at all.
I don't have an attitude problem. You have a perception problem.
Do not walk behind me; I may not lead. Do not walk ahead of me; I may not
    follow. Do not walk beside me, either; just leave me alone!
In some cultures, I would be considered normal.
Ten million sperm and YOU were the fastest?

Others in Your Life
Happiness is having a loving and caring family in another city.
Coming from a dysfunctional family doesn't entitle you to be a serial killer.
If marriages were outlawed, only outlaws would have in-laws.
Never underestimate the power of stupid people in large groups.
Controlling myself is almost as good as controlling others.
Never go to bed mad. Stay up and fight.
It is much easier to apologize than to ask permission.
Love your neighbor... but don't get caught.

Love and Happiness
Love may be blind, but marriage is a real eye-opener.
You cannot make someone love you, but you can make them pay.
If you love something, set it free. If it doesn't come back, hunt it down, kill it.
Sex without love is an empty experience; but as empty experiences go, it's one
    of the best. (Woody Allen)
Sex is not the answer. Sex is the question. "Yes" is the answer.
Happiness is following the teachings of Christ as long as they don't interfere
    with your favorite vices.
If ignorance is bliss, you must be orgasmic.
Pain and suffering is inevitable, but misery is optional.
Beware of people who smile excessively.
The secret of a happy marriage remains a secret.
If you are afraid of loneliness, don't marry. (Anton Chekhov)

Body, Mind, and Soul
Beauty is skin deep; ugly goes right to the bone.
In the dark, all people are beautiful.
Young at heart, slightly older in other places.
Lord, if I can't be skinny, please let all my friends be fat.
When I die, I'm leaving my body to science fiction. (Steven Wright)
It is easier to get older than it is to get wiser.
I went to school to become a wit, but I only got half-way through.
Of all the things I've lost, I miss my mind the most.
Please, Lord, let me prove that winning the lottery won't spoil me.
Hello, Front Desk? Some guy named Gideon left his Bible here.
Trust in God but lock your door.
The more you complain, the longer God lets you live.
I lost my faith in nihilism.

Values, Mission, and Vision
Give a man a fish and he'll eat for a day. Teach him how to fish and he'll sit in
    the boat and drink beer all day.
...teach him to fish, and he'll overfish, cause famine in the next three
    regions, and pollute the atmosphere with his fish.
A clear conscience is usually the sign of a bad memory.
We are all in the gutter, but some are looking at the stars. (Oscar Wilde)
Money is a poor way of keeping score if you're losing.
Experience is something you don't get until just after you need it.
When I get to where I'm going, will somebody please tell me where I am?
In two days, tomorrow will be yesterday.
Old age and treachery will beat youth and skill every time.
The only thing we have to fear is fear itself—but let's not overlook fear.
Modesty is a vastly overrated virtue. (J. K. Galbraith)
Those are my principles. If you don't like them, I have others. (G. Marx)
Abstain from wine, women, and song... mostly song.

Tactics
Never put off until tomorrow what you can avoid doing altogether.
I don't have a solution, but I admire your problem.
For every action there is an equal and opposite criticism.
He who hesitates is probably right.
Two wrongs are only the beginning.
Hard work pays off in the future; laziness pays off now.
If you try to fail and succeed, what have you done?
I have not yet begun to procrastinate.
When you wrestle with a pig in the mud, notice that he's enjoying it.
Things to do today: see list of things to do yesterday.

Eagles may soar, but weasels aren't sucked into jet engines.
No problem is so formidable that you can't walk away from it. (C. Schulz)
Only put off until tomorrow that which you are willing to leave undone when you die. (Pablo Picasso)

Success
If at first you don't succeed...

> ...sky-diving is not for you.
> ... destroy all the evidence that you tried.
> ... the heck with it.
> ... find out if the loser gets everything.

If at first you do succeed, try not to look astonished.
If you do it right the first time, nobody appreciates how difficult it was.
Success always occurs in private, failure in full view.
It's not whether you win or lose, but how you place the blame.
The sooner I get discouraged and quit, the more time I'll save overall. (Frank Sergeant)
If everything seems to be going well, you have obviously overlooked something. (Steven Wright)
It was so different before everything changed.

Life and Death
The Senility Prayer:

> God grant me the Senility
> To forget the people I never liked anyway
> The good fortune to run into the ones I do
> And the eyesight to tell the difference.

All reports are in. Life is now officially unfair.
Nostalgia isn't what it used to be.
Just because you're paranoid doesn't mean they are not out to get you.
The problem with the gene pool is that there is no lifeguard.
Someday we'll look back at this, laugh nervously, and change the subject.
I used to have a handle on life, but it broke.
Life is sexually transmitted.
Death is life's way of telling you you've been fired.
Sooner or later, everyone stops smoking.
Those who live by the sword get shot by those who don't.

Journey into the Self
To enter one's own self, it is necessary to go armed to the teeth. (Paul Valery)
We are all serving a life sentence in the dungeon of the Self. (Cyril Connolly)

Glossary

Portions adapted from *The Concise Columbia Encyclopedia* and *The American Heritage® Dictionary of the English Language, Third Edition.*

altruism: Unselfish concern for the good of others.

Aristotle: (384-322 B.C.) Ancient Greek philosopher whose philosophical theory follows empirical observation and logic and is the essential method of rational inquiry. Aristotle is well-known for his **Nicomachean Ethics**.

behavior modification: The use of basic learning techniques to alter human behavior.

behavior therapy: The use of basic learning techniques to modify toxic behavior patterns by substituting new responses to given stimuli for undesirable ones.

egoism: The ethical doctrine that morality has its foundations in self-interest, and that self-interest is the just and proper motive for all human conduct.

ethics: Principles of right conduct; a system of moral values.

extroversion and introversion: Carl Jung's classification of two basic psychological types. While a person can enjoy aspects of either, Jung believed a person tends to lean more strongly one way than the other. The extrovert is directed toward the outside world and is happiest with other people and with activity. The introvert prefers solitude and the inner life.

goals: The end towards which effort is directed.

Hedonism: The doctrine that postulates that only that which is pleasant, or has pleasant consequences, is fundamentally good.

honesty: the quality or condition of being truthful or sincere

integrity: Strict adherence to a moral or ethical code

libertarian: One who believes in freedom of action and thought or in free will.

morality: The quality of being in accord with the standards of a system of right or good conduct.

Nicomachean Ethics: A list of twelve basic virtues postulated by **Aristotle**. He notes that if any virtue is excessive of or deficient from its mean level, it becomes a vice to be avoided.

objectivism: Philosophical doctrine holding that all reality is objective and external to the mind and that knowledge is reliably based on observed objects and events.

pleasure principle: In psychoanalysis, the tendency or drive to achieve pleasure and avoid pain as the chief motivating force in behavior.

psychopath and sociopath: A psychopath is a person affected by an antisocial personality disorder, especially one manifested in perverted, criminal, or amoral behavior. A sociopath is antisocial and may also be aggressive.

Rand, Ayn: (1905-1982) Russian-born American writer whose works defended political conservatism and **objectivism**.

strategy: The science of planning and directing large-scale military operations, of maneuvering forces into the most advantageous position prior to actual engagement of the enemy. It asks, "What should be done?"

Stoicism: The pantheist doctrine that postulates that all reality is material but is shaped by a universal force (God) that in found in all things.

tactics: The science or art of disposing military and naval forces in action before an enemy; any skillful management for effecting a desired result. It answers, "How should the task be done?"

Bibliography and Other Selections in My Library

The following authors and their books were used as reference material when writing *Optimize Your Life!*, or their works have been inspirational to my Mission and Vision. Where possible, author web sites are given.

Armstrong, Karen, *A History of God,* 1993 (Alfred A. Knopf, Inc./Ballantine)

Blair, Gary Ryan, "The GoalsGuy" - GoalsGuy.com

Boldt, Laurence G., *Zen and the Art of Making a Living,* 1991 (Penguin Arkana) - EmpowerYou.com

Bolles, Richard Nelson, *What Color is Your Parachute?,* 2002 (Ten Speed Press) - JobHuntersBible.com

Boorstin, Daniel J., *The Discoverers,* 1983 (Random House); *The Creators,* 1992 (Vintage Books); and *The Seekers,* 1998 (Random House)

Britannica Great Books (54 books), *Great Books of the Western World,* 1952 (University of Chicago)

Bunyan, John, *The Pilgrim's Progress,* 1902 (Lothrop)

Campbell, Joseph, *The Hero with a Thousand Faces,* 1949 (Bollingen Series XVII, Princeton University Press) and *The Mythic Image,* 1974 (Princeton University Press)

Capra, Fritjof, *The Tao of Physics,* 1975, 1983, 1991 (Third Edition, Updated, Shambhala Publications) - FritjofCapra.net

Covey, Dr. Stephen R., *The 7 Habits of Highly Effective People,* 1989 (Fireside/Simon & Schuster) and *The 8th Habit: From Effectiveness to Greatness,* 2004 (Free Press/Simon & Schuster) - StephenCovey.com

Durant, Will, *The Story of Civilization Parts I-X,* 1939, 1966 (Simon & Schuster)

Flanigan, Beverly, M.S.S.W., *Forgiving Yourself,* 1996 (Macmillan/Simon & Schuster)

Frager, Robert, Ph.D., *Who Am I? Personality Types for Self-Discovery,* 1994 (G.P. Putnam's Sons)

Fromm, Erich, *To Have or To Be?* 1976 (Bantam)

Goodstein, Leonard D.; Nolan, Timothy M.; and Pfeiffer, J. William, *Applied Strategic Planning: A Comprehensive Guide,* 1993 (McGraw-Hill) and *Plan or Die!* 1993 (Pfeiffer and Company)

Hall, Doug, with Wecker, Dave, *Jump Start Your Brain,* 1995 (Warner Books)

Hansen, Mark Victor, et al., *Chicken Soup for the Soul* series (HCI)

Huang, Chungliang Al, *Quantum Soup,* 1991 (Celestial Arts) LivingTao.com

Kirschenbaum, Dr. Howard, Simon, Dr. Sidney B., and Howe, Dr. Leland W., *Values Clarification,* 1972-1995 (Warner Books); Kirschenbaum, Dr. Howard, *Advanced Value Clarification,* 1977 (Pfeiffer & Co.) - SimonWorkshops.com; www.rochester.edu/Warner/faculty/kirschenbaum

Koberg, Don, and Bagnall, Jim, *The Universal Traveler,* 1991 (Crisp Publications)

Inlow, Dr. Linda C. Beattie, *Becoming ME,* 1998 (Kopacetic Ink)

Lewis, C.S., *Mere Christianity,* 1943, 1945, 1952 (The Macmillan Company)

Maslow, Abraham H., *Religions, Values, and Peak-Experiences,* 1970 (Viking Penguin)

McWilliams, Peter and John-Roger, *Do It! Let's Get Off Our Buts* and *Life 101: Everything We Wish We Had Learned About Life in School—But Didn't,* 1991 (Prelude Press) - McWilliams.com

Mintzberg, Henry, *The Rise and Fall of Strategic Planning,* 1994 (The Free Press/Simon & Schuster) - HenryMintzberg.com

Morrisey, George L., *Creating Your Future: Personal Strategic Planning for Professionals,* 1992 (First Edition, Berrett-Koehler) and the *Morrisey on Planning* series, 1995 (Jossey-Bass) - Morrisey.com

Moses, et al., *The Holy Bible,* 1445 BC—95 AD (?)- UnboundBible.org

Nanus, Burt, *Visionary Leadership,* 1995 (Jossey-Bass) and *Leaders Who Make a Difference,* 1999 (Jossey-Bass)

Peck, M. Scott, M.D., *The Road Less Traveled,* 1978; *The Road Less Traveled and Beyond,* and *Further Along the Road Less Traveled,* 1993 (Touchstone/Simon & Schuster) - MScottPeck.com

Porter, Michael E., *Competitive Strategy,* 1980 (The Free Press/Macmillan Publishing Co.)

Qubein, Nido, *Stairway to Success,* 1996 (Wiley) and *How to Be a Great Communicator,* 1997 (Wiley)

Rand, Ayn, *The Virtue of Selfishness,* 1961 (Signet/New American Library/Penguin Putnam)

Reiss, Steven, Ph.D., *Who Am I? The 16 Basic Desires That Motivate Our Actions and Define Our Personalities,* 2000 (Berkley/Penguin Putnam)

Ringer, Robert J., *Looking Out for #1,* 1977 (Fawcett Crest) - RobertRinger.com

Tzu, Lao, *Tao Te Ching: About the Way of Nature and Its Powers (Thomas J. Miles Translation),* 1992 (Avery Publishing Group Inc.)

Von Oech, Roger, *A Whack on the Side of the Head,* 1983 (Warner Books) and *A Kick in the Seat of the Pants,* 1986 (HarperPerennial) - CreativeThink.com

Waitley, Denis, *The Psychology of Winning,* 1992 (Berkley Publishing Group) - www.Waitley.com

Watts, Alan, *The Way of Zen,* 1957, 1985 (Vintage/Random House)

* * *

Some very useful publications for lifetime management are offered by Bottom Line Secrets, 281 Tresser Boulevard, 8th Floor, Stamford, CT 06901-3246, BottomLineSecrets.com. They offer monthly publications including Bottom Line/Personal, Bottom Line/Tomorrow, Bottom Line/Health, and Tax Hotline, as well as yearbooks.

Saluting Our Cartoonists

Charles Barsotti is a thirty year veteran signature cartoonist of *The New Yorker*. His simple but elegant style is featured in *The Essential Charles Barsotti* compiled by Lee Lorenz including over 150 of his best cartoons.
www.Barsotti.com

Chunkit Cheung began his career in a computer game company working on animations. He owns and operates his U.K.-based company Dragoncraft, wherein he creates illustrations and comic books.
www.dragoncraft.freeservers.com

Cathy Guisewite's comic strip *Cathy* debuted in 1976. It currently appears in more than 1,400 newspapers worldwide. In addition, more than twenty collections and gift books of *Cathy* cartoons have been published.
www.UComics.com/cathy

Bruce Eric Kaplan's droll wit has been seen in his regular cartoons in *The New Yorker* and his book, *No One You Know*. He has also written for series television *including Seinfeld, Cybill, The Naked Truth,* and *Six Feet Under.*
www.CartoonBank.com

Robert Mankoff is a very successful cartoonist and president of The Cartoon Bank. He has been the Cartoon Editor at *The New Yorker since 1997*. He has published *E-Mail This Book.*
www.CartoonBank.com

J. Ira Monroe is nationally published in the U.S. and U.K. in the children's educational market. As the "Bwana" Greeting Card Company, he produces cartoon cards with outlets in the U.S. and

Australia.
www.bwanaart.tripod.com

Ashok Rajagopalan was born in a mountain village in India in 1964. He has been a freelance cartoonist, illustrator, art director, and art teacher since 1989. He is working on comic stories and was recently published in *Chatterbox* in India.
www.ashokraj.itgo.com

Paul Taylor has been a professional cartoonist since 1982. He has been published worldwide in magazines and tabloids ranging from *Private Eye* to *The Spectator* to *Punch.*
www.CartoonResource.com

Sir John Tenniel (1820-1914) is most famous for his illustrations in Lewis Carroll's *Alice in Wonderland* and *Through the Looking Glass.* Well known for his political cartoons, this English carica-turist was often seen in the legendary *Punch* (1851-1901).
www.Punch.co.uk

Cathy Thorne's cartoons are simple line drawings coupled with warm, amusing, reflective captions, which are products of her as-tute observations. Based in Toronto, her Everyday People car-toons appear in newspapers, magazines, books, and greeting cards.
www.EverydayPeopleCartoons.com

Andrew Toos was raised on a farm in the Amish country of Pennsylvania. His cartoons are known to readers of *Saturday Eve-ning Post, CEO, Barron's, The New Yorker,* and hundreds of other publications, but he is better known as the poet and writer, Andrew Grossman.
www.CartoonResource.com

Web Sites
Some current, interesting Internet sites.
(Note: sites come... sites go.)

Self
www.Self.com
www.SelfGrowth.com
www.NASE.com

Philosophy
www.utm.edu/research/IEP
www.Plato.Stanford.edu
www.PhilosophyPages.com
www.SamKeen.com
www.JimRohn.com
www.AynRand.com
www.Yogi-Berra.com

Religion
www.ChristianityToday.com
www.Islam.org
www.Jewish.com
www.Scientology.org
www.RetreatsIntl.org
www.RetreatsOnline.com
www.DeepakChopra.com
www.Atheists.org

Psychology Tests
www.EnneagramInstitute.com
www.QueenDom.com
www.AdvisorTcam.com
www.HighlandsPrograms.com
www.OutofService.com
www.MentorU.com
www.CareerCC.org

Body, Mind, and Soul
www.SoulHealer.com
www.MindBodySoul.gov.uk

www.Guidance.com
www.TheDailyGuru.com

Values
www.ForBetterLife.org
www.ValuesoftheWise.com
www.PersonalValues.com

Quotations
www.QuotationsPage.com
www.QuoteLand.com
www.CreativeQuotations.com
www.Murphys-Laws.com

General Resources
www.Pueblo.GSA.gov
www.GovernmentGuide.com
www.BrianTracy.com
www.MarkVictorHansen.com
www.EmpowerMe.com
www.EmpowerYou.com

Death
www.HolisticMed.com
www.Hemlock.org

Success/Life Management
www.AnthonyRobbins.com
www.FranklinCovey.com
www.BottomLineSecrets.com

Other
www.EthicalWill.com
www.SJDM.org
www.Questia.com
www.CoachU.com

List of Competencies

Personal Skills (Self)	
Ambition	Information management
Analyzing	Learning
Artistic talents	Logical reasoning
Athletics	Musical talents
Carpentry	Organizing
Computer skills	Persistence
Cooking	Planning
Creative thinking	Reading
Decision making	Self-motivating
Discipline	Sewing
Driving	Solving Problems
Financial management	Time management
Fishing	Typing
Gardening	Visualizing
Hunting	

Interpersonal Skills (Others)	
Brainstorming	Leading
Coaching	Listening
Collaborating	Mentoring
Communicating (verbal)	Motivating
Communicating (written)	Multi-tasking
Conflict resolution	Negotiating
Coordinating	Networking
Counseling	Persuading
Delegating	Public speaking
Facilitating	Teaching
Flexibility	Team building

"'Tis God gives skill, but not without men's hands:
He could not make Antonio Stradivari's violins without Antonio."
—George Eliot

It's Feedback, Testimonial, and Follow-up Time

This book was written for *you*.

You are encouraged to send comments, pithy or sarcastic quotations, ideas, and personal stories about yourself.

I would like to hear from you as to how this book has helped you... or *not*.

You can contact me via:
DrBDahl@aol.com

...or you can enter a message on the Web site:
www.TrionicsUSA.com/oyl

...or write to me at:
Bernhoff A. Dahl, M.D.
66 Upper Oak Point
Winterport, ME 04496

* * *

We are interested in clever and short "mottoes for life," such as:

"Work hard
Make a profit
Have fun."
—Sinclair Lewis, *Babbitt*

"Live fast, love hard..."

Send us your favorite motto, either from literature or lyrics, or your own creative mind.

About the Author: Bernhoff A. Dahl, M.D.

I was born and raised in northern New Jersey, the son of Norwegian immigrants. Since my father was self-employed in manufacturing and real estate, I enjoyed a good, albeit hectic, life. I was a hyperkinetic kid and a good student with too many interests and projects.

In my efforts to gain some control and focus over these many projects, I discovered the power of color-coded file folders. Later, I graduated to three-ring notebooks.

For me, life had followed an orderly and efficient series of phases. I was raised in a conservative, fundamentalist Baptist church, and then went on to Wheaton College in Illinois (Reverend Billy Graham's alma mater) where I earned degrees in Chemistry and Bible. Next I went to Cornell University Medical College for my M.D. and completed my internship and Pathology residency at the University of Vermont.

In 1971, after two years as an Epidemic Intelligence Service officer with the Center for Disease Control in Atlanta, I was named the Chief of Pathology at Eastern Maine Medical Center in Bangor, Maine.

As a result of my early life and religious upbringing, as well as my formal education as a chemist, an epidemiologist, and a physician/pathologist, my world view was as wide as possible. My interests and knowledge ranged from chemical elements and tissue cells to celestial beings (*aka* God), from disease processes in individuals to health concerns of large populations. I was steeped in Aristotelian logic and philosophy, as well as the scientific method.

However, since my four years at Cornell included a great deal of training in psychiatry, my religious concepts were tested and molded. I was comfortable in the world of the abstract, unseen, untested, and unproven.

In Maine, I co-founded Dahl-Chase Pathology Associates (DCPA) which served eighteen hospitals and three reference labs in the state. During the next twenty-five years of "in the trenches" medical group practice, I learned a great deal. I was forced to address the complex nature of people, especially myself, as we struggled to succeed.

These experiences led me to the study, understanding, and application of the benefits of the dynamic management tool, strategic planning. I have applied strategic planning to countless management venues, both inside and outside the practice of medicine, as an owner, co-owner, and consultant.

In 1995, I retired from the full-time practice of pathology and founded PathQuest, Inc., a management consultancy. Over the years, I have offered lectures, seminars, and consultation services on leadership issues and skills with a focus on strategic planning.

For additional insights into my personal Mission, Vision, and Values, you are cordially invited to visit my Web site at:

www.DrBDahl.com

The author gaining wisdom and knowledge from the Oracle at Delphi.

Pythia—the Oracle at Delphi—claimed that Socrates was the wisest man in the world, much to Socrates' annoyance. He had proclaimed that he actually knew nothing. He finally realized the wisdom of the Oracle: by claiming to know nothing, he was, perhaps, the wisest of men.

The author, trying to be clever, proclaimed his ignorance to the Oracle. The Oracle simply agreed.

"I believe that any man's life will be filled with constant and unexpected encouragement, if he makes up his mind to do his level best each day, and as nearly as possible reaching the high water mark of pure and useful living."
—Booker T. Washington

"Great things are not done by impulse, but by a series of small things brought together."
—Vincent Van Gogh

"We will either find a way or we will make one."
—Hannibal

Also by Bernhoff A. Dahl, M.D., books for organizational strategic thinking and planning:

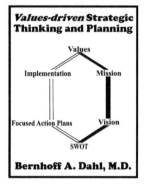

Values-driven Strategic Thinking and Planning

Values-driven Strategic Thinking and Planning addresses the principles and practices of full-scale Strategic Planning. It is extremely user-friendly and is easy to understand and implement.

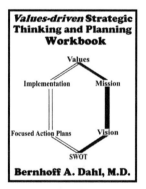

Values-driven Strategic Thinking and Planning Workbook

A perfect companion to the *Values-driven* book, this is a complete facilitator-friendly workbook, with worksheets designed to assist a facilitator in guiding the participants of an organization, group, or team as they address the STP process.

Visit www.TrionicsUSA.com/vdstp

Index

SPECIAL ORDER FORM

You are encouraged to order additional copies of the book
Optimize Your Life! Interactive Worksheets CD Edition
from your favorite local or online bookstore. Apellicon-Pearson Press
offers the following direct order services:

Fax Orders: 207-848-5649 (send this form)
Online Orders: www.TrionicsUSA.com/oyl
Postal Orders: Send this form to:

Bernhoff A. Dahl, M.D.
Trionics International Inc.
66 Upper Oak Point
Winterport, ME 04496 USA

Please send _____ copies of *Optimize Your Life! Interactive Work-*
sheets CD Edition @ $19.95 per copy for a total of $_____.
(Maine residents add sales tax.)

Shipping

- **USPS Book Rate:** $3.00 first book, $2.00 each additional.
- **USPS Priority:** $5.00 first book, $3.00 each additional.
- **International:** $9.00 first book, $5.00 each additional.

TOTAL OF THIS ORDER: $_____

Name: _____
Address: _____
City: _____ **State:** _____ **Zip:** _____
Telephone: _____
Email: _____

Payment

___**Check: $** _____ ___**Money Order: $** _____
___**Credit Card $** _____ **:**
___**Visa** ___**Master Card** ___**AmEx** ___**Discover**
Card number: _____
Name on Card: _____ **Exp. Date:** _____

> **Special Pricing: This book is available at a volume discount**
> **for educational use, employee gifts, sales promotions, premiums,**
> **fund-raising, or reselling. Custom-printed editions, too.**

Please send more FREE information on:
___**Other Books** ___**Speaking/Workshops** ___**Consulting**

Optimize Your Life!
Interactive Worksheets CD

There are over 40 worksheets contained in the book. While you are welcome to photocopy and enlarge the worksheets to fill out by hand, they're all provided in full 8.5" x 11" size on the included Interactive Worksheets CD included inside the back cover. Using the Interactive Worksheets, you can print out these full-size versions and thereby gain more room to write.

Go interactive! But of Interactive Worksheets are exactly what they sound like—*interactive!* They're in PDF format and each sheet is form-fillable, meaning you can click your mouse in them and type up your personal planning information.

How it works. By using either the Adobe Acrobat full version software, or using the Adobe Reader with the CutePDF Form Filler software for Windows users, you can enter, change, edit, save, print, and password protect your personal planning. Instead of writing it out once and having to write it all over again later, you can load in your Interactive Worksheets with all your data and make any changes, additions, and deletions you like. It's a great way to keep your personal planning organized!

Included software. Windows version of Adobe Reader and CutePDF Form Filler are included on the CD. Macintosh users without the full version of Adobe Acrobat, or without compatible software allowing them to save form-filled data, will not be able to save entered data.

E-Book, too! Also included on the CD is an e-Book version of *Optimize Your Life!* for easy, quick reference on your computer.

Need more information? To get started, put in the CD and view the text and PDF instruction files.